AN ENVIRONMENT
ANCIENT GREEC

MW00476326

In ancient Greece and Rome an ambiguous relationship developed between man and nature, and this decisively determined the manner in which they treated the environment. On the one hand, nature was conceived as a space characterised and inhabited by divine powers, which deserved appropriate respect. On the other, a rationalist view emerged, according to which humans were to subdue nature using their technologies and to dispose of its resources. This book systematically describes the ways in which the Greeks and Romans intervened in the environment and thus traces the history of the tension between the exploitation of resources and the protection of nature, from early Greece to the period of late antiquity. At the same time, it analyses the comprehensive opening up of the Mediterranean and the northern frontier regions, both for settlement and for economic activity. The book's level and approach make it highly accessible to students and non-specialists.

LUKAS THOMMEN is a professor in the Historical Institute at the University of Zurich and is also a member of the Sosipolis International Institute of Ancient Hellenic History in Greece.

AN ENVIRONMENTAL HISTORY OF ANCIENT GREECE AND ROME

LUKAS THOMMEN

TRANSLATED BY

PHILIP HILL

CAMBRIDGE
UNIVERSITY PRESS

CAMBRIDGE
UNIVERSITY PRESS

University Printing House, Cambridge CB2 8BS, United Kingdom

One Liberty Plaza, 20th Floor, New York, NY 10006, USA

477 Williamstown Road, Port Melbourne, VIC 3207, Australia

314-321, 3rd Floor, Plot 3, Splendor Forum, Jasola District Centre, New Delhi - 110025, India

79 Anson Road, #06-04/06, Singapore 079906

Cambridge University Press is part of the University of Cambridge.

It furthers the University's mission by disseminating knowledge in the pursuit of
education, learning and research at the highest international levels of excellence.

www.cambridge.org
Information on this title: www.cambridge.org/9780521174657

Originally Published in German by Verlag C.H. Beck oHG, München 2009 as
Umweltgeschichte der Antike by Lukas Thommen

© Verlag C.H. Beck oHG, München 2009

Revised English edition first published 2012

A catalogue record for this publication is available from the British Library

Library of Congress Cataloging in Publication data
Thommen, Lukas.
[Umweltgeschichte der Antike. English]
An environmental history of ancient Greece and Rome / Lukas Thommen;
translated by Philip Hill. – Rev. English ed.
p. cm.
"Originally published in German by Verlag C.H. Beck . . . München, 2009,
as Umweltgeschichte der Antike"–T.p. verso.
Based on Umweltgeschichte der Antike, somewhat expanded and with chapter 22,
The environment in Roman Britain, added.
Includes bibliographical references and index.
ISBN 978-1-107-00216-6 (Hardback) – ISBN 978-0-521-17465-7 (Paperback)
1. Human ecology–Greece–History–To 1500. 2. Human ecology–Rome–History.
3. Greece–History–146 B.C.–323 A.D. 4. Rome–History–Republic, 265–30 B.C.
5. Rome–History–Empire, 30 B.C.–284 A.D. 6. Greece–Environmental conditions.
7. Rome–Environmental conditions. I. Title.
GF13.3.G74T4713 2012
304.20938–dc23
2011030736

ISBN 978-1-107-00216-6 Hardback
ISBN 978-0-521-17465-7 Paperback

Contents

Figures

Preface

This book is based on my *Umweltgeschichte der Antike* (Munich: C.H. Beck, 2009), somewhat expanded and with the new Chapter 22, 'The environment in Roman Britain', added. It goes back to my many years of teaching environmental history at the University of Basel (1995–2005), and attempts to convey the foundations for historical research on the environment in the ancient world. I hope that it can thus serve as a point of departure for further study of the topic.

I would like to thank Paul Cartledge and Peter Garnsey for their useful comments, as well as Michael Sharp for editing the manuscript with the kind assistance of Josephine Lane and Merle Read. I am also indebted to the Freiwillige Akademische Gesellschaft (Voluntary Academic Society) of Basel for providing a significant contribution toward the cost of the translation, and to Philip Hill (Berlin), for carrying out that work.

Introduction

In view of the environmental problems of our own time, we are increasingly addressing the question of the historical roots and conditions of ecological crises. This leads us back far beyond the environmental history of the past fifty years, and addresses long-term developments of human history since the earliest times. It also includes a large number of scientific disciplines: prehistory, history, geography, geology, anthropology, medicine, biology, ethnology and others. Clearly, environmental historical work relying on a single discipline would be inadequate or too one-sided; it would need to be completed by results from other fields of study, and, ideally, meshed with them. *interdisciplinary*

Ancient history as a discipline draws primarily on the literary sources, from Greece of the archaic era through to late antiquity. It thus addresses primarily ancient perceptions, descriptions and interpretations, which risks a one-dimensional perspective. For a more adequate reconstruction of ancient environmental conditions, this volume will attempt to at least begin to include research from other disciplines, even if no comprehensive interdisciplinary approach can as yet be realised.

The primary goal of the study of antiquity must be the examination of the peculiarities of human behaviour under the specific conditions prevailing at the time in question. The assessment of ancient conceptions of the environment or ancient environmental behaviour in terms of modern standards is problematical from the outset. Broad-brush prejudices, which either paint a picture of an idyllic ancient world where humankind and nature were one, or else go to the other extreme to emphasise the scant respect for nature exhibited by the Greeks and Romans, are in fact not particularly helpful in this regard. The number and scope of impacts are generally of entirely different dimensions than is the case today, and are based on very different technological and societal foundations. A reconstruction of ancient conditions can therefore contribute only indirectly to enlarging our field of vision for an analysis of our own time.

I

The most conspicuous interventions of the Greeks in nature were first of all forest clearing and mining, as well as the common wartime tactic of devastating the enemy's farmland to rob him of his sustenance, at least temporarily. The realisation that forest clearing led to soil erosion, and hence to the loss of farm and pastureland, quickly gained acceptance, but this was apparently not accompanied by any fundamental critique of clear-cutting. Clearing the forest was seen first and foremost as part of the progress of civilisation – as it would be later, too, among the Romans. On the other hand, the damage to farmland was probably of limited scale, neither leading to immediate shortages nor providing any comprehensive picture of the finiteness of resources. The Greeks and Romans of course still lacked the technological wherewithal to inflict global damage upon the environment. They thus never faced the necessity of fundamentally reconsidering their behaviour towards nature.

The numerous foundations of cities in countries all around the Mediterranean, which began during the first millennium BC, constituted a fundamental intervention in the landscape. Even in archaic times (between the eighth century BC and 500 BC) considerable quantities of stone, wood and metal were needed for public and private buildings. The temples, theatres, columned halls and gymnasia – schools for both athletic and artistic education – of the classical era (500–336 BC) demanded still more materials, and were the cause of even greater degrees of overexploitation, yet they also led to various forms of reuse and recycling. Certainly, the splendour and pomposity of the Hellenistic royal courts demonstrates that the ancient Greeks did not always husband natural resources in a thrifty manner, nor did their impacts upon nature exclusively result from the purposes of satisfying basic needs. This does, however, appear to some extent as a contradiction to their fundamental religious beliefs, according to which they venerated 'Mother Earth' in the form of the goddess Demeter, and always appreciated the beauty of pleasant groves, bays and river landscapes.

The Romans were able to expand still further the range of impacts on nature, both in the countryside and in the towns, and even to extend it north of the Alps, to large areas of Europe. Even in pre-imperial times, Rome was already confronted with urban problems not unfamiliar to us today. Congested streets, traffic noise, the stench of waste, and plumes of smoke from charcoal heating and baths led to a deterioration in living conditions, particularly of the lower classes of society. Huge numbers of exotic wild animals died in bloodthirsty public spectacles in the arenas, on a scale which threatened a number of species, such as the hippopotamus in

Lower Egypt, with extinction in some areas. While there was sporadic criticism of damage to nature caused by rapacious mining or the popular practice of lining rivers and lake shores with villas, this criticism was aimed less at the destruction of the environment than at the material greed and addiction to splendour for which the upper classes were thus berated.

The carelessness of the ancients in their stewardship of nature and its raw materials has certainly had its effects. The impacts of the utilisation of nature and the landscape in ancient times were considerable in many areas. Both southern and northern Europe, which was then newly incorporated into the ancient civilisational realm, were transformed. Nevertheless, popular opinion, according to which the widespread karst formation in various areas of the Mediterranean is due to clear-cutting of forests in ancient times, turns out to be wrong. Caution is called for when interpreting ancient intervention in nature, for in many areas later natural or anthropogenic changes, such as the building of the Venetian fleet or clear-cutting during the nineteenth century, have contributed to today's appearance of the landscape.

The discussion of humankind and the environment in antiquity necessarily makes use of modern terms for environmental phenomena, which are, however, associated with particular periods of history and hence require clarification as to their origins and meanings. This moreover includes the term 'environmental history' itself, the contents and approaches of which have to be placed in a history-of-science perspective; moreover, its relevance or applicability to antiquity must first be examined. In this context, reference must be made to the research both of modern and of ancient environmental history, so as to delimit the scope of the study.

TERMINOLOGY

Neither ancient Greek nor Latin had words for many of the concepts familiar to us today in connection with environmental issues – the word 'environment' itself heads the list. That does not necessarily mean that there was no such thing as environmental awareness in antiquity. It does, however, show that the Greeks and Romans had a different conception of quite a number of phenomena, and that this fact influenced their behaviour towards the environment, and towards nature – for which they did develop a specific term. Let us then examine the origins and the meaning of the particularly important terms *nature, the environment, climate, ecology, sustainability, disaster* and *waste,* and how the content of those

Connection ↑ to themes

terms was described in the age of antiquity. That will itself reveal some characteristic basic attitudes of the Greeks and Romans in their dealing with their environment.

Nature actually means 'that which has come into being or has grown without outside assistance', and is derived from the Latin *natura*, which means 'bringing forth'. The term is a translation of the Greek word *physis*, which describes both the creative force of nature and the natural order, and the natural essence of an object or of a living being. Nature as a space in its own right is in fact a discovery of the Greeks, who, in the context of the emergence of politically autonomous communities (*poleis*; sing.: *polis*), defined it as that which excluded their own achievements, the sum of which constituted 'culture' (*nomos*); this emphasised the value of the latter. However, they also realised that a mere dichotomy of nature vs culture – or *physis* vs *nomos* – was a false assumption, since they were to an extent interdependent, and the human, as a component of transitory nature, affected its processes (Plat. *leg.* 890d, 903c: humankind is not made for its own sake, but for the natural whole). Despite the consciousness of human superiority and achievement which emerged in antiquity, there also existed the demand to allow the *physis* the freedom to run its course, and to follow nature and live in harmony with it (Diog. Laert. 7.87ff.; Stob. 2.75ff.; Sen. *epist.* 122.19).

From the sixth century BC the Greeks in various cities along the coast of Asia Minor began to investigate the basic materials and laws of nature. These elements, they believed, were in constant change, so that nature could be seen as undergoing a process. By contrast with our own times, science in antiquity by and large did without experimentation, and engaged instead in the observation (*theoria*) of the cosmos as an ideal, predestined order. However, despite this rationality with which nature's substances and processes were thus permeated, the need remained to venerate nature religiously. So, as we shall see, the relationship of the Greeks and Romans to nature presented no uniform overall picture; rather, it included elements both of the veneration and of the domination of nature. As the term 'nature' had no specific association with protecting the environment, humans had considerable freedom in how they acted.

The English word *environment* came into common use in the early nineteenth century as a translation of the German words *Umgebung* – today usually translated as 'surroundings' – and *Umwelt*, the modern word for 'environment'. The latter is attested since 1800, and means literally 'surrounding country' or 'surrounding world'. By the second half of the nineteenth century it had in Germany replaced the French word *milieu* as the term for the realm in which life arises and carries on.[1] In the biological sense, *Umwelt* was first used by the Baltic German biologist Jacob von Uexküll in 1909 to mean the surroundings of a living being, which affect that being and influence its conditions of life.[2] Since that time, the concept of *Umwelt* or 'environment' has been further developed scientifically, and is today seen as 'the world surrounding humankind', as the sum of all phenomena which influence the life situation of a human community.[3] In that sense, it is an anthropocentric concept, according to which nature serves humankind. However, the word has since the late 1950s also acquired an ecological, scientific application with regard to environmental protection. Only since the 1970s has an inflationary use of the term been observable, so that '*Umwelt*/environment' has now degenerated to an empty phrase, a shell.

Thus, there was no distinct term for 'environment' in antiquity; it was incorporated in the concept of *physis*. Environment in the modern sense was only characterised at a general level, at which primarily such climatic factors as wind and water were taken into account. *To periechon* in ancient Greece generally meant 'that which surrounds' the earth, and which could also be seen as a mixture of celestial phenomena, in effect as the climate. *Klima*, in Greek and Latin, means the curvature of the earth and describes the celestial realm, as a geographical location and zone (Strab. 2.1.35, 5.34). In reference to climate, ancient texts generally speak about the 'air', which could have various temperatures and currents, and could also be considerably affected by waters, the rain and the condition of the ground, a prominent example being Hippocrates' *On Airs, Waters, and Places* (Hippocr. *aër.* 1). Here, he uses neither the term *periechon* nor *klima*; he does, however, distinguish between European and Asiatic climatic zones, to which he attributes a decisive influence on human physical – and political – constitutions. As this concept was more of general theoretical character, a term for the environment itself was not required.

The environmental determinism established by the Greeks was also adopted by the Romans, albeit with Rome now replacing Athens as the centre of ideal environmental conditions (Vitr. 3.9–10). Pliny the Elder observed the effects of the soil and the climate in the form of the 'sky' (*caelus*) on the trees, which, he claimed, loved the north wind the most, as they grew thicker and stronger under its influence (*nat.* 17.9–10).

---

[1] Fuchsloch 1996, 4.
[2] Jacob von Uexküll, *Umwelt und Innenwelt der Tiere*, Berlin, 1909.
[3] Winiwarter 1994, 131, 154; cf. Merchant 1993, 1.

The environment was thus analysed pragmatically, with an eye to economic gain, and at the same time reduced to certain external phenomena, and used for political propaganda. No comprehensive, systematic discussion of environmental factors occurred, so that neither any real concept of the environment nor any profound ecological studies emerged.

The concept of *ecology* (German *Ökologie*) is of more recent vintage, and is the product of the scientific research of the nineteenth century. In 1866 the German natural scientist Ernst Haeckel described the *Umwelt* (environment) as the 'surrounding outside world', and defined the concept of ecology as 'the body of knowledge concerning the economy of nature – the total relations of the animal to both its inorganic and organic environment, including in the broader sense all "conditions of existence"'.[4] He saw ecology as a complete science which included all factors surrounding an organism, and interpreted it as part of the surrounding system. To this day, ecology is still the 'interdisciplinary scientific study of the interactions between organisms and their environment', but also 'of the distribution and abundance of organisms and the interactions that determine distribution and abundance'.[5] Ecology is also the study of ecosystems, which describe the web of relations among organisms at various scales of organisation.

While the term 'ecology' is derived from the Greek, it is notable that it did not exist in antiquity. *Oikos* means 'house' or 'the household', and by derivation, its budget, so that *oikonomia*/economy means the science and the laws of budget management, from which modern economics is derived. The word combination *oikologia* connects *oikos* with *logos*, rationality or intellect, and thus describes a kind of budget science of nature. In antiquity there were only modest initial approaches towards this concept.

The philosopher Theophrastus (*c.* 370–287 BC) for example determined the climatic zones in which certain plants were indigenous, and diagnosed climatic changes due to certain interventions in nature (*caus. plant.* 5.14.2–3). In Roman times Pausanias ascertained that the Meander (the Menderes in modern Turkey), which flowed through the cultivated country of the Phrygians and Carians, and therefore carried a large quantity of sediments, was silting up the bay between Priene and Miletus into which it emptied, while the Achelous, which flowed through the deserted country of the Aetolians, did not carry any comparable amount of silt (8.24.11; cf. 7.2.10–11). Nevertheless, the Echinades islands off its

---

[4] Ernst Haeckel, *Generelle Morphologie der Organismen*, Berlin, 1866, II.286, I.8.
[5] Begon et al. 2006, xi.

mouth were partially silted up (Hdt. 2.10; Thuc. 2.102), so neither was more reliable information available in this area, nor were more detailed investigations undertaken. Important observations of the human influence on habitat were widespread, yet more weight was given – not only terminologically – to economy than ecology, which was not yet established as a subject of research in its own right.

Only thanks to the knowledge of modern ecology did the demand for 'sustainability' or 'sustainable activity' emerge during the late twentieth century. *Sustainability* and *sustainable* as a concept are a creation of the 1970s, derived from the Latin *sustinere,* 'to uphold'. The English word includes two key concepts, that of being able to bear a load and that of being able to continue at a certain level over time; it is also used in the term 'sustainable growth'.[6] (The German word *Nachhaltigkeit* is derived from *Nachhalt,* which originally meant something to be stored for hard times. It is first attested in 1713, and was used in the area of forestry,[7] and came into general usage around 1800. The German word conveys only the second of the two meanings of its English equivalent, so that there are instances in which 'sustainable' is translated into German as *zukunfts-fähig* – literally 'future-capable'.)

Strictly speaking, the concept of sustainability demands that only such a quantity of energy and raw materials be used as will be restored through natural processes during the same period. Moreover, only as many pollutants may be passed on to the environment as it can cope with during the same time period. The term 'sustainability' came into widespread use especially as a result of the UN's Brundtland Commission Report of 1987, the *Report of the World Commission on Environment and Development: Our Common Future,* which contained the following definition: 'Sustainable development is development that meets the needs of the present without compromising the ability of future generations to meet their own needs.' Unlike traditional concepts of environmental protection, sustainable development tries to incorporate existing social needs adequately. However, this also risks diminishing or neglecting negative impacts upon nature. In today's parlance, moreover, 'sustainable' often loses any direct reference to environmental issues, and is used in all kinds of contexts to simply mean 'effective in the longer term' or 'long-lasting', and hence 'high quality'.

[6] *Online Etymology Dictionary,* s.v. 'sustainable', http://www.etymonline.com/index.php?search=sustainable&searchmode=none.

[7] Hanns Carl von Carlowitz, *Sylvicultura Oeconomica (Anweisung zur wilden Baum-Zucht),* Leipzig, 1713.

The demand that raw material extraction be restricted to the renewable products of the earth's surface was already formulated by Pliny the Elder in the first century AD, albeit more as a moral appeal than as a conservationist demand (*nat.* 33.1ff.). Faith in the infinity of resources, or the regenerability both of surface and subsurface materials, was dominant (Xen. *vect.* 1.4, 4.2ff.; Strab. 3.2.8–10). The ancients had not yet addressed the issue of the planned management and distribution of resources, and thus could develop no real concept of sustainability. The question, too, of equal access to goods and social justice was completely beyond the pale.

Disaster comes from the Italian *disastro*, 'ill-starred', a calamity due to an unfavourable planetary position. 'Hazard' means a threatening calamity stemming from nature, while 'disaster' describes natural phenomena which become a catastrophe only owing to the vulnerability of society; A. Oliver-Smith speaks of 'failures of human systems'.[8] 'A disaster is the tragedy of a natural or human-made hazard (a hazard is a situation which poses a level of threat to life, health, property, or environment) that negatively affects society or environment ... disasters are seen as the consequence of inappropriately managed risk.'[9] In German, *Katastrophe* simply means a serious accident, generally sudden and unexpected, which causes major damage and requires outside help. The problem there is the question of predictability, as well as the subjective and objective effects of the event on people and/or the environment, and the question of dealing with the event. Modern catastrophe research therefore addresses the natural and social conditions existing prior to extreme events, while also analysing the actual process and the consequences, according to certain patterns. People in antiquity were still a long way from any such considerations, inasmuch as divination (fortune-telling) was the principle strategy and form of communication with the environment, and allowed no effective access to catastrophic contingencies.

Catastrophe in Greek and Latin means a reversal, an unexpected change, but did not refer explicitly to nature. Natural devastation was seen as misfortunate and ruinous – *kakon* (Dio 77.2), *pestis* (Tac. *ann.* 2.47), *clades* (Sen. *nat.* 6.2.9) – and a divine punishment for bad moral behaviour (Cic. *nat. deor.* 2.14; Plin. *nat.* 33.1–2). In Seneca's view, natural events such as catastrophic floods occurred according to a predefined plan which humans could hardly counteract (*nat.* 3.27.1ff.). Scientific

---

[8] Oliver-Smith and Hoffman 1999, 28.
[9] Popular definition in *Wikipedia*, s.v. 'disaster', http://en.wikipedia.org/wiki/Disaster (16 January 2006).

investigations into the natural causes of such events, modest as they were, concentrated on supposed underground winds, fires and waters. Both precautionary measures and rescue strategies were conceived only rudimentarily. In classical times Greek cities helped each other out during catastrophes; in the Hellenistic period the kings emerged as the major donors at such times, and such activity then became a regular task of the Roman emperors.[10] Nevertheless, a largely fatalistic attitude prevailed in this area throughout antiquity. There was a readiness to suffer the vagaries of nature and its hazards, since they were seen as possessing an overarching significance.

Waste is from the Latin *vastus* (bleak, barren, void) and refers to unusable or unwanted material. This has become a growing problem only with the age of industrialisation, since the nineteenth century. Since the 1950s the rubbish of consumer society has been added to the problem, giving rise to the recycling of materials and the energy contained in them. In antiquity certain craft products were indeed already manufactured serially in industrial production; nonetheless, waste in the modern sense was still unknown. Accordingly, only early forms of recycling emerged, primarily the reuse of materials which were either valuable or of limited availability, such as metals, stone blocks and timber. Even in classical Greece such non-degradable substances as ceramic fragments ended up in rubbish pits and landfill deposits.

The Greek word for waste is *apostasis*, meaning abandonment of a political faction or regime. Otherwise, waste products are known only from handicrafts, under product-specific names – such as the waste products of sawing, wood-carving or planing. There were, however, several terms for trash (*skybala, skoria, pelos*). *Kopros* describes dung and fertiliser, and faeces and dirt. For the Romans the only term other than those for the waste products of crafts was *stercus*, which can be translated as 'dirt', and also includes faeces in the form of dung and fertiliser. Urine was collected in the city of Rome and used by fullers for leather processing, while animal dung was used in the countryside as fertiliser. In addition, efforts were undertaken at various places to remove filth from residential settlement areas under the supervision of officials. Much waste was nevertheless left lying around in ancient cities, often resulting in their contamination and pollution on a scale which no modern concept of hygiene would tolerate.

[10] Meißner 2008.

MODERN ENVIRONMENTAL HISTORY: THEORETICAL
APPROACHES AND PERIODISATION

Environmental research is altogether a relatively young field of science which emerged as a significant force only as a result of the ecological crisis of the 1960s. Nonetheless, environmental history has to this day remained largely a 'fringe area' of historical research. It is far better established in the United States than in Europe, particularly thanks to the work of Donald Worster (*Nature's Economy. A History of Ecological Ideas*, 1977), William Cronon (*Changes in the Land. Indians, Colonists and the Ecology of New England*, 1983) and Alfred W. Crosby (*Ecological Imperialism. The Biological Expansion of Europe 900–1900*, 1986) and to the journal *Environmental History*. The continental, particularly the German-speaking, discourse was long dominated by a more technological-historical approach, but is now broadly diversified and integrated through the European Society for Environmental History, founded in 1999. Rolf Peter Sieferle (*Rückblick auf die Natur* ['A look back at nature'], 1997) provides a comprehensive system-theoretical approach. Christian Pfister has distinguished himself in the field of historical climate research (*Wetternachhersage* ['Weather post-diction'], 1999). J. Donald Hughes (*What is Environmental History?*, 2006) and more recently Verena Winiwarter and Martin Knoll (*Umweltgeschichte* ['Environmental history'], 2007) have provided introductory overviews.

Environmental history examines the past interaction between people and the rest of nature, that is, the environmental conditions which prevailed in the past, and their perception and interpretation by contemporaries:[11]

> The object of environmental history is the social and economic dimension of human communities with respect to interactions in a habitat ... The 'environment' in environmental history is thus all phenomena which influence the life situation of a human community. It takes into account all human actions which have any effect – even indirect – on the resource base and the natural spatial surroundings.[12]

In J. D. Hughes's view, there are three main areas of environmental historical interest which apply to all epochs of world history:

(1) the influence of environmental factors on human history; (2) the environmental changes caused by human actions, and the many ways in which human-caused

---

[11] Hughes 2001, 4–5; Hughes 2006, 1; Winiwarter and Knoll 2007, 14–15.
[12] Winiwarter 1994, 154.

changes in the environment rebound and affect the course of change in human societies; and (3) the history of human thought about the environment and the ways in which patterns of human attitudes have motivated actions that affect the environment.[13]

Furthermore, R. P. Sieferle points out:

'Environmental history' therefore deals in principle with a difficult, tortuous process: it reconstructs a complex interaction between human cultures and their natural environment, and must integrate both perspectives in the process. It must not only ask – as the older environmental determinism has done – whether and to what extent natural conditions affect societal processes ... What should become clear are the basic conditions established by natural circumstances, which scope of action existed for cultural-societal self-organisation, and how the limits which nature placed on society were constituted.[14]

Integral environmental history strives for a comprehensive reconstruction of the human-environmental relationship. Also useful in this respect is the 'environmental hygiene' approach, which examines the effects of culture on 'harmonious' nature, and thus arrives in the proximity of social history.

According to V. Winiwarter, the environment can be subdivided into various subsystems, the specific place and time relationship of which provides information about the prevailing environmental conditions:[15]

1. The material environment: the material conditions of the habitat, such as the availability and quality of water; the climate; the types and conditions of the soil; the infrastructure; and the availability of natural resources such as wood, building materials, mineral resources etc.
2. The structural environment: the possibilities and conditions for the utilisation of the material environment; the relations of ownership; the availability of technology for the exploitation of natural resources; the basic legal, political and economic conditions.
3. The intellectual environment: the possibilities and conditions for human access to phenomena, such as a concept of nature; the religion; the technical and philosophical level of knowledge.

Since, according to Immanuel Kant, the human being is the object of study of the science of history, the concept of the environment in environmental history is anthropocentric: history – that which has occurred – is of relevance only for those who write about it or study it. The bio-eco-systemic approach can, according to Winiwarter, be incorporated as

---

[13] Hughes 2006, 3.   [14] Sieferle 1997, 13–14.   [15] Winiwarter 1994, 155.

an important aspect; however, it is not constitutive: 'The object of historical environmental research is the extrapolation of scientific data sets into the past', which involves such methods as climatic history, pollen analysis and dendrochronology (the calculation of the felling date of trees using their growth rings).[16] According to Sieferle, the 'human ecological perspectives' of historical environmental research include energy flows, material cycles, population, pathogens and the effects of industrialisation.[17] Historical ecology pursues the goal of using knowledge of the current situation for the study of the environment in the past. As ecology 'includes social and cultural patterns', ecological history is 'somewhat broader than environmental history, but the two terms often are used interchangeably'.[18]

Basically, Sieferle argues, three factors of the investigation of environment history can be ascertained:[19] 'Nature', or natural ecosystems; 'human population' in the physical sense; and 'culture' as an organisational pattern. Four areas of work emerge from this: the reconstruction of particular systems of culture and nature in the past; the stability and duration of the respective system of culture and nature; the periodisation of environmental history, with explanations of the transitions; and finally the history of pollution. The problem overall is the consequences of human behaviour from a long-term perspective, which must be investigated using an interdisciplinary approach.

In environmental history a rough periodisation has gained acceptance in which the periods correspond both to energy systems and to landscape types:[20] first are the Palaeolithic hunter and gatherer societies up to 12,000 years ago, which lived in a natural landscape without the cultivation of natural products. With the end of the last ice age, the Neolithic revolution began over 10,000 years ago, bringing with it a radical upheaval which began in the Fertile Crescent approximately 8,000 years ago and was characterised by agriculture, sedentary life and the domestication of animals. The changes led to the emergence of agrarian societies, with the use of solar energy and natural energy flows in cultivated landscape. Here a distinction is made between the peasant societies prior to the emergence of advanced civilisations, roughly 5,000 years ago, and the stage of these agrarian-based civilisations. Finally, after a long interval, came the period of industrialisation, which began more than 200 years ago. It led to the consumption of fossil sources of energy with high energy flows in an initially segmented, later 'total' industry landscape. At first,

---

[16] Winiwarter 1994, 154–5.   [17] Sieferle 1988, 311ff.   [18] Merchant 1993, 1.   [19] Sieferle 1993.
[20] Simmons 1993, 1ff.; Sieferle 1993, 1995, 1997.

coal was the central energy source; thereafter, the use of oil and natural gas became virtually universal. The city walls had long been torn down; now the cities lost their ties to their surrounding countryside, and mobility grew constantly. The resulting consumer society was accompanied by a massive drop in the price of fossil energy sources during the 1950s.[21]

Ancient societies were thus fundamentally tied to agriculture, and dependent on natural energy. Water power was used largely for mills; wind power only for sailing ships. Petroleum and bituminous and brown coal were known but were not widely used, and played no role for energy supply. The primary fuels used were wood, charcoal and olive oil for lamps, so that renewable energy sources predominated. Nevertheless, cases of resource depletion were recorded, in terms of timber construction, mining and land use. These instances were, however, hardly perceived as alarm signals – unlike the situation today – and could often be compensated for by opening up new lands.

ANCIENT ENVIRONMENTAL HISTORY: A REVIEW

Despite the topicality of environmental history over the past three decades or more, ecological research on ancient times is still in its nascent stage. The full-scale results of geological and botanical investigations are still pending; moreover, the periodisation of environmental history needs to be further refined, and differentiated spatially and chronologically. The reconstruction of natural zones, material cycles and ecosystems is limited as a result of the paucity of sources. Historians investigating antiquity from an ecological scientific perspective have very restricted data and other means at their disposal. The material remains allow only limited conclusions to be drawn, and the documentary sources often support only indirect conclusions about conditions in ancient times. To date, few coherent discussions of humankind and the environment in antiquity exist.

Russell Meiggs set an initial milestone with his work *Trees and Timber in the Ancient Mediterranean World* (1982). Robin Osborne then provided an updated form of regional studies: *Classical Landscape with Figures: The Ancient Greek City and Its Countryside* (1987), which was followed by Robert Sallares' extensive work *The Ecology of the Ancient Greek World* (1991), which sought explanations for cultural development in climatic and biological developments, including domestication. With *Smog über*

---

[21] Pfister 1995.

Attika (1990), Karl-Wilhelm Weeber provided a popular scientific summary of ancient environmental problems. Paolo Fedeli presented a comprehensive depiction of the Roman situation, *La natura violata: ecologia e mondo romano*, also in 1990. A useful source book on the environment of the Graeco-Roman world is Giangiacomo Panessa's *Fonti greche e latine per la storia dell'ambiente e del clima nel mondo greco* ('Greek and Latin sources on the history of the environment and the climate in the Greek world', 1991).

Weeber's introductory work was complemented by J. Donald Hughes's comprehensive *Pan's Travail: Environmental Problems of the Ancient Greeks and Romans* (1994), by Günther E. Thüry's *Die Wurzeln unserer Umweltkrise und die griechisch-römische Antike* ('The roots of our environmental crisis and Graeco-Roman antiquity', 1995), and by Gudrun Vögler's *Öko-Griechen und grüne Römer?* ('Eco-Greeks and green Romans?', 1997). In 1999 Holger Sonnabend published both a description of 'natural disasters of antiquity' (*Naturkatastrophen in der Antike*) and a dictionary of 'people and landscapes in antiquity' (*Mensch und Landschaft in der Antike*), many of the entries in which provide useful introductions and references to secondary sources.

Like the modern concept of ecology generally, these recent representations are based on initial examinations from the nineteenth and early twentieth centuries. The conditions of life and customs of the Greeks and Romans, as well as their relationship to nature, were already addressed in the great treatises on the 'private/home life' of the ancients (German *Sittengeschichte*, 'moral history'), albeit with no basis in natural-scientific examination.[22] At that time, such topics familiar in our own time as food, bathing and personal hygiene, lumber supply and horticulture were already addressed comprehensively. On the other hand, ancient geography also enjoyed great popularity. Heinrich Nissen's *Italische Landeskunde* ('Italic geographic studies', 1883–1902) was a notable work on Roman geography, while Alfred Philippson and Ernst Kirsten wrote a similar book on Greece, *Die griechischen Landschaften* ('The Greek landscapes', 4 vols., 1950–9), which is still useful to this day, and has never really been surpassed.

A pioneering work on the ancient environment was *The Geography of the Mediterranean Region: Its Relation to Ancient History* by Ellen C. Semple (1931). More recently, Hansjörg Küster's *Geschichte der Landschaft in Mitteleuropa* ('History of the landscape in central Europe', 1995)

---

[22] Marquardt 1886; Blümner 1911; Friedlaender 1921–3.

is a chronological and geographical overview which also takes the ancient period into account. Peregrine Horden and Nicholas Purcell emphasise in *The Corrupting Sea: A Study of Mediterranean History* (2000) that the pre-modern Mediterranean is typified by an exceptional 'fragmentation' of 'microregions' and inconstant 'microecologies', where risk is managed by traditionally high 'connectivity'. Their work has been followed by the overviews of Alfred T. Grove and Oliver Rackham, *The Nature of Mediterranean Europe: An Ecological History* (2001), and J. Donald Hughes, *The Mediterranean: An Environmental History* (2005).

THE GOAL OF THIS BOOK

The present book on the one hand addresses the foundations which determined the relationship between humankind and nature in Graeco-Roman antiquity. It thus attempts to ascertain the interactive complexes of effects between people and their environment during the period starting with the early Greeks – the ninth to eighth centuries BC – up through late antiquity, or the fourth to fifth centuries AD. The first factors to be taken into account are the geographical space and the ancient understanding of nature. The latter includes both mythical interpretations and the proto-scientific view of the world: its four elements, water, earth, fire and air; the theory of climatic determinism, according to which the physical constitution and the political system were influenced by the climate; and the manner in which animals and plants were dealt with.

On the other hand, this book seeks to examine concrete aspects in the relationship between humans and the environment in greater detail. These aspects include various human interventions in nature, such as farming and food procurement, forest cover and timber construction, the destruction of nature in war, horticulture, hydraulic construction, mining and urban problems. Finally, it investigates changes in nature and seeks to determine their significance for ancient society: the shift of coastlines and the siltation of river mouths, and such extreme events as conflagrations, earthquakes, volcanic eruptions and floods.

The book comprises two parts, 'Greece' and 'Rome', and is largely structured with parallel chapters, so as to show both the similarities and the differences between the two civilisations and their handling of nature. The ancient Mediterranean world is thus not treated as a geographically closed space in a historically uniform era, but rather subdivided into two cultures, with partly different chronologies. In addition, the chapter on

Roman Britain, a regional study of a geographically more limited land-scape, compiles the issues and problems addressed in an exemplary summary.

This book is based for the most part on the literary sources, which are inserted into the text in brackets; thus, ancient perceptions inevitably move into the foreground. Natural-scientific investigations of various types which are increasingly contributing results to problems of ancient history can be taken into account only to a limited degree, and these methods are not discussed in detail. The examined areas therefore do not cover the full range of environmental issues, but are rather to a large degree determined by the literary material. The multi-layered problem of diseases and epidemics – together with very uncertain population statistics – can be, for example, only marginally addressed.

Furthermore, owing to the uneven availability of sources, it is hardly ever possible to always examine the contents presented according to a uniform structure of questions. It is the task of the historian to arrange the environmental phenomena addressed in their intellectual and cultural context, and to investigate the different results. In that way, the dependence of ancient society on the environment is to be highlighted, and a contribution provided to an understanding of the culture of that era. In this respect, environmental history can be understood as a part of general history, and can serve the purpose of opening up a view of ancient civilisation so as to create a reference to the foundations which have permanently shaped the people and landscape of Europe, and which, with manifold breaks, have remained effective up to our own time.

Historians today are called upon to contribute to a critical dealing with nature and hence, too, to engage in environmental research. This book seeks to do so by conveying the basis for historical research in the field of the environment in antiquity, and to provide a point of departure for further investigation of this topic in the future. For this purpose, it also includes detailed secondary bibliographical references for each chapter, and a short bibliographical essay at the end of the book.

PART I
Greece

CHAPTER I

The geographic space

Ancient Greece encompassed the southern part of the Balkan peninsula and the Peloponnese, as well as the numerous islands of the Aegean Sea and the more remote islands of Crete and Cyprus. Moreover, Greek cities were founded along the adjacent coast of Asia Minor, in modern Turkey, during the early part of the first millennium BC. Finally, during the colonisation period starting in the second half of the eighth century BC, Greek settlements sprang up all round the Mediterranean and to some extent even on the Black Sea. This far-flung urban construction constituted the most important transformation of the landscape in the ancient world, and the one with the most lasting consequences.

Both geographical and political factors were decisive in the emergence of this Greek world. The landscape of Greece itself, with its small-scale structures, has only a few broad coastal strips and fertile plains, but many promontories and offshore islands. The resulting landscape pockets are separated from one another by numerous mountain ranges and bays which cut deep into the coastline, so that fragmentation is the most striking characteristic (Fig. 1). Nevertheless, in the valleys and small plains conducive to settlement and farming, humus-rich areas were formed from the soil washed down from the mountains. Politically, the decisive factor was that after the decline of the great castles and palaces such as Mycenae, Tiryns and Pylos around 1200 BC, the fall in population in the ensuing period and the beginning of settlement activity in the early years of the first millennium BC, there was no threat from the outside, kingship had disappeared and an autonomous development of small communities was able to emerge. There were very few common, supraregional tasks which had to be addressed.

Despite the early voyages of discovery, commercial relations and the founding of cities, geographical knowledge remained modest until Hellenistic times (336–30 BC). The earth was thought to be flat, surrounded by the Okeanos, the world-embracing ocean, and subdivided

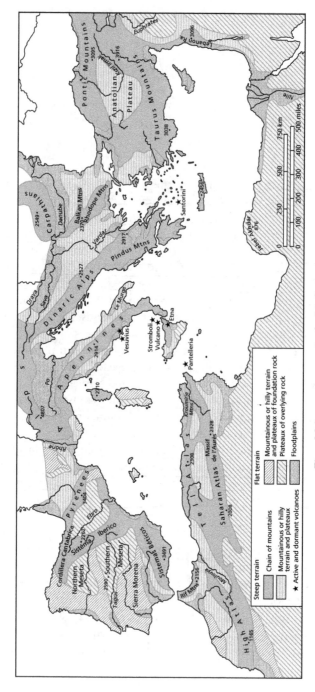

Fig. 1 Major terrain types in the Mediterranean area.

by seas and rivers. The natural philosopher Anaximander of Miletus drew
the first map of the world in the sixth century BC; it was improved upon
by Hecataeus, who added a description of the earth (*Periodos ges*). Around
the time of the transition to the classical era, the idea that the world was
round first emerged, and in the third century BC Eratosthenes was even
able to attempt a measurement of it, although that did not put the notion
that it was flat to rest. After 326 BC, when the Macedonian king Alexander
the Great reached the Indus on his campaign of conquest in Asia, and was
there faced with the realisation that the end of the inhabited world was
not discernible, the 'conquerability' of the entire earth was seriously called
into question – even if the Romans would later repeatedly consider that
prospect.

THE 'POLIS' AND THE 'CHORA': THE CITY AND ITS COUNTRYSIDE

The form of community and state organisation characteristic of the Greek
world was what we describe as the *polis*, or city state. *Polis* originally meant
castle or fortress, and by extension also referred to the settlement under
the protection of that fortification. Hence, *polis* meant both the city and
the city state, the community of citizens, a community united around a
municipal centre with its surrounding countryside (*chora*), managing itself
autonomously and protecting the landed property of its members. There
thus emerged a pattern of fortified centres and unfortified rural settlements near to cultivated fields; densely populated landscapes concentrated
administrative, religious and political functions in a municipal centre. In
the case of Athens, interior settlement has been observed in the *polis*
territory, with a number of villages being established in the countryside
surrounding the city.[1] Despite the dominance of a centre, no polarisation
arose between town and country, as the city's residents too were often
farmers. Altogether, we can assume some 700 *poleis* in the Greek world.
A *polis* often had only several hundred citizens, although in the case of
Athens, approximately 30,000 citizens enjoyed full political rights;
beyond that, the city was home to an equal number of metics – foreign
residents without Athenian citizenship rights – and slaves. Since these
figures refer only to adult males, the full population of Athens was about
50,000, with around 250,000 as a whole in the region of Attica (there was
no legal urban–rural distinction).

[1] Zimmermann 2004, 131.

The *polis* first arose in the ninth or eighth century BC; the first literary testimonials to it are from Homer and Hesiod around 700 BC. The planning of the settlements was oriented around a centre, the *agora*, which served as a market and meeting place, with public buildings. Temples are already provable in the tenth century BC, as in Aigeira in the northern Peloponnese. Central cults emerged, connecting the newly established communities. For political purposes, the citizens assembled on the *agorai*, which were ever more frequently used. In Athens the municipal centre apparently initially lay to the north-east of the Acropolis. Further west, in the area of the future *agora*, which first had to be drained, were graves dating back to the eighth century BC. Thereafter, a cemetery was established outside the settlement (the Kerameikos; see Fig. 7 below).

A network of long-distance routes already existed at the time of the Greek *poleis*, that is, not merely regional roads or processional ways to such shrines as Eleusis or Delphi. These consisted primarily of footpaths or single-track roads for wagon traffic, which have particularly been ascertained in the Peloponnese.[2] Strabo (5.3.8) generally tells of unpaved roads without drainage ditches. However, this deficiency hardly impeded local trade or export-oriented large-scale production. A lively trade existed even in early times, for the sea especially provided regular connections between particular regions and remote areas.

THE ERA OF COLONISATION

The Greek settlement had considerable implications for the landscape of southern Europe up to the area of the Black Sea. After the second half of the eighth century BC, the Greek world included areas all around the Mediterranean, so that the Greeks lived 'like ants or frogs around a marsh' (Plat. *Phaid.* 109b). The colonists were driven both by such crises as population growth, scarcity of farmland, the fragmentation of holdings and political disputes, and by the eagerness to discover new geographical areas and peoples. The Greeks called their colonies *apoikiai*, or 'outward (re)settlements', in which the settlers built new lives for themselves.

This was, however, only possible where there were both suitable vegetation and sufficient arable land to provide self-sufficiency. In areas dominated or controlled by major powers, only trading stations could be established. Such outposts were built in Syria (Al Mina, Tell Sukas), starting in the eighth century BC, and after the sixth century BC also in

[2] Tausend 2006.

Egypt (Naukratis), Spain (Ampurias/Emporion) and Etruria (Spina, Pyrgoi), where primarily metals but also luxury goods were obtained. In the other direction, Greek products such as the bronze *krater* ('vessel') of Vix reached the Celts in Gaul and the adjacent areas of central Europe by way of the Phocaean colony of Massilia (Marseilles) at the mouth of the Rhone.

The colonisation often proceeded by first taking possession of an offshore island, from which the occupation of the mainland could then be carried out. This procedure could already be observed in the earliest colonies in southern Italy – such as Pithecusae on the island of Ischia, which preceded the founding of Cumae – and in Sicily, and also in North Africa (Cyrene in Libya). The towns were planned with a grid of right-angled streets, public squares and shrines. The urban builder Hippodamus of Miletus took up this form during the fifth century BC and attained fame for it, so that similar settlements arose in many places in the Greek world.

Unlike their modern counterparts, these colonies were independent of their mother cities, and were not subordinate to any imperial nation-state striving for control of large territories. Nonetheless, as in modern times, the colonies often exported raw materials and in return purchased such finished products as ceramic vessels and other artisans' wares. Starting from the coastal settlements, land was occupied and raw materials extracted in the hinterland. In that way, new farmland was developed, parcelled out and cultivated, as can be seen in Metapontum in southern Italy.[3] One negative result of the expansion of settlement activity in some places was the siltation of river mouths, such as that of the Meander at Miletus, particularly after the third century BC. However, cultivation and terracing could also check erosion, as the example of Olympia suggests (see below).

THE HELLENISTIC KINGDOMS

With the conquests of Alexander the Great of Macedonia (336–323 BC), the area in which the Greeks settled and into which they carried their culture was enlarged considerably, for the entire Near East and Egypt came under the control of Macedonian kings. During his campaign against the Persians, Alexander had himself founded numerous cities, all the way to Baktria and Sogdia (modern Afghanistan and Tajikistan) and

[3] Mertens 2006, 332–3.

also on the Indus. Alexandria, which he built in Egypt, became the first multi-functional urban centre, serving political-administrative, military and economic purposes, and with the Museion, a research institute, became a new scientific centre. The offshore island of Pharos was connected with the mainland by an artificial causeway, so that two new harbour basins were created, and the landscape was changed extensively by technical means.

The great Hellenistic kingships of the Macedonians, Ptolemies and Seleucids which succeeded Alexander's reign promoted intensive internal colonising activities. Dozens of new towns which were Greek by culture sprang up in Asia Minor and in the Near East, in which Greek and Macedonian veterans were settled and given land grants in the surrounding countryside. Moreover, older settlements were refounded or Hellenised; here, the Greek gymnasium performed a key function as a seat of learning. The Seleucids established four important cities in Syria between the Mediterranean and Mesopotamia – Antioch, Apamea, and the ports of Seleucia Pieria and Laodicea – through which the fertile country along the Orontes was opened up and the northern Levantine coast kept under control. Originally, Seleucia on the Tigris near Babylon had been built as the royal residence and new capital of the Seleucid kingdom, but this was then transferred to Antioch on the Orontes. As a result, Antioch developed into a trade and cultural centre famous for its urban luxury, including water pipes and street lighting, and for the parks in the Grove of Apollo, in the suburb of Daphne.

Here the kings controlled not only the political, military and administrative structures; they also had vast landholdings in these enormous kingdoms. They demanded taxes in money and in kind from their subjects and tenants, so that intensive farming of the soil was initiated. In the Egyptian *chora* and in southern Syria, Ptolemaic soldiers were even issued landholdings, which they could lease out during campaigns, and later even sell.[4] While some of the large Hellenistic empires soon began to crumble as a result of their many conflicts with one another, their era was only definitely brought to an end by the Romans, who subjugated the remaining kingdoms, Macedonia, Asia Minor, Syria and Egypt, as well as all of Greece, to their rule between 148 and 30 BC. This at the same time guaranteed settlement continuity and a gradual transition from Greek to Roman habits and legal structures.

---

[4] Cohen 1978, 53ff., 63ff.

CLIMATE, COASTLINES AND ESTUARIES

As part of the newly developed art of investigation of natural history, the Greek philosopher Parmenides in the first half of the fifth century BC divided the earth into climatic zones for the first time, broadly distinguishing the scorched south, the temperate Mediterranean zone and the frigid north (Strab. 2.2.2). In the text attributed to him *On Airs, Waters, and Places*, the Greek physician Hippocrates of Kos (*c.* 460–370 BC) distinguished primarily between European and Asiatic climatic zones, which, he believed, had shaped the people quite differently. Aristotle in the fourth century BC enlarged the conventional number of four winds – Boreas, Zephyros, Euros and Notos – to eight, and initially occupied himself with meteorology. Later, his system was further differentiated (Plin. *nat.* 2.119ff.). Eratosthenes, who in Alexandria in the third century BC first measured the globe, distinguished seven climatic zones in parallel strips. This, however, hardly expanded geographical knowledge significantly, nor was climatic determinism questioned. No concrete effects of this teaching on settlement activity are apparent.

In addition to literary sources, scientific research into the climate and the landscape in antiquity is particularly important; of course, it has only been carried out for a few regions. Moreover, the human influence on the climate in antiquity is generally very difficult to discern. Overall, the climate apparently remained relatively constant after the ninth century BC, generally marked in the Mediterranean area by mild, rainy winters and hot, dry summers. A climatically colder and wetter period has been established between 850 and 600 BC, and again in the fourth century BC,[5] primarily using carbon dating (the C^{14} curve) and Greenland ice-core analysis (the $\delta^{18}O$ curve). In the second century BC a drier and warmer phase began,[6] which is also attested by the agricultural writer Saserna (Colum. 1.1.4–5). Nevertheless, it is not clear whether this was continuous, or whether increased precipitation and a temperature drop should be assumed, as glacier growth may indicate.[7] Ice-core data reveal that from AD 145 to 185 cold winters but also warm and damp summers predominated, until an overall deterioration finally began in the third century AD.[8] In North Africa and the Iberian peninsula we can assume, for the period of the Roman occupation, a higher level of precipitation, which had a positive effect on economic development.

---

[5] Maise 1998, 219–20.   [6] Lamb 1981; cf. Chapter 22, n. 2, below.
[7] Patzelt 1994; Nenninger 2001, 98.   [8] Klostermann 2008, 29–30.

Even in the early phase (*c.* 50,000–10,000 BC), a filling of the river valleys with sediments can be ascertained all around the Mediterranean ('Older Fill'); it can be attributed to climatic changes. Additional layers, starting in late antiquity at the latest and continuing to modern times ('Younger Fill'), have also been deposited.[9] These were in some cases already initiated substantially earlier, even in the Bronze Age, and may be due not only to climatic but also to anthropogenic causes.[10] Despite numerous uncertainties, regional scientific studies should be able to clarify the differences in the effects caused by civilisation.

Four phases can be distinguished in the area of the Gulf of Taranto (Basilicata and Lucania), into which several parallel rivers flow. In a first phase beginning approximately 11,700 years ago, during the late Pleistocene and early Holocene, climatically caused deposits appear. During the next three phases, the Graeco-Roman period, the Middle Ages and the last two centuries, human influence becomes obvious in the sediments, indicating deforestation and agriculture.[11] In the Argolis on the Peloponnese, river sediments show an early Bronze Age fill, with no further deposits until the Hellenistic period. This can be explained in part through terrace and dam construction, which was neglected again later.[12] The settlement of Olympia was abandoned in the fifth century AD, and was gradually covered by a 10 m thick layer of sediment from the rivers Kladeos and Alpheios,[13] although here anthropogenic influence was probably not the only cause.[14]

In addition to climatic and human impact, the sea level and the shorelines are also factors affecting the areas adjacent to the Mediterranean. In ancient times the sea level was approximately 1.5 to 2 m lower than it is today; it has been rising gradually with the melting of polar and other glaciers. Especially in the western Mediterranean, therefore, ancient shorelines are often now flooded; such cities as Larymna on the Gulf of Atalanti in central Greece and the part of Cyme in western Asia Minor which faced the sea are now under water.[15] However, the rising of the sea level was also accompanied by horizontal coastal movement and increasing sedimentation of the rivers. The ports of Delos and the Libyan ports in Sabratha, Leptis Magna (Fig. 2) and Apollonia are all now silted up,[16] as are Ostia, Sybaris and Metapontum. While Kenchreai, the eastern port of Corinth, was disappearing into the sea, Helike on the Gulf of Corinth

[9] Vita-Finzi 1969.   [10] Wagstaff 1981.   [11] Brückner 1983, 1986, 1990.
[12] Van Andel et al. 1986, 1990.   [13] Büdel 1981, 259ff.   [14] Grove and Rackham 2001, 291ff.
[15] Schäfer and Simon 1981, 29.   [16] Trousset 1987, 137ff.

Fig. 2 Silted harbour of Leptis Magna, Libya.

was struck by an earthquake and tsunami in 373 BC, and possibly buried under the sediments of three rivers.

Alluvia caused by humans and reinforced by the climate led to the widespread problem of the siltation of river mouths, as in the cases of the Nile, the Meander, the Achelous, the Po, the Tiber, the Rhone and the Ebro. The historian Thucydides (2.102) reported that the Achelous, separating the regions of Acarnania and Aetolia in western Greece, dumped a considerable amount of material in winter, and that some of the Echinades islands lying off its mouth had already been silted up. The Gulf of Thessalonika (Gulf of Therma) silted up between 500 BC and AD 100, so that only a small inland lake was left.[17] Since there are no major rivers in Greece, it was the river mouths of Asia Minor, such as the Cayster (Ephesus) and the Meander (Miletus, Heraclea, Myus), which were affected most drastically by siltation.

Our main source for the mouth of the Meander at the Gulf of Latmos is Pausanias (second century AD, 7.2.10–11):

The people of Myus left their city on account of the following accident. A small inlet of the sea used to run into their land. This inlet the River Meander turned into a lake, by blocking up the entrance with mud. When the water, ceasing to be sea, became fresh, gnats in vast swarms bred in the lake until the inhabitants were forced to leave the city. They departed for Miletus, taking with them the images of the gods and their other movables, and on my visit I found nothing in Myus except a white marble temple of Dionysus. (Loeb)

Though in the fifth century BC the port of Myus had still been used by warships (Hdt. 5.36), by the first century BC the city could be reached

<hr/>

[17] Eumorphopulos 1963; Bintliff 1981, 18.

through the muddy water only by rowing boats, while Priene, to the north-west, was entirely silted up at a distance of 40 stadia (*c.* 7.5 km); further south, however, Heraclea was apparently still located on the sea coast (Strab. 12.8.17, 14.1.8, 10). By the first century AD the Meander was reported to have emptied into the sea 10 stadia (*c.* 1.85 km) from Miletus (Plin. *nat.* 5.113), so that the siltation had progressed at an average of approximately 2 km per century – considerably faster than siltation at the Cayster had done at Ephesus. By the fourth century AD, the ports of Miletus seem to have been entirely silted up, and later accessible only by way of the Meander, although the speed of siltation decreased considerably after the end of antiquity.[18]

[18] Brückner 1997.

CHAPTER 2

People and nature

The issue of environmental behaviour necessarily raises questions about the opinions and images that ancient people had of nature generally. It appears that the Greeks' relationship with nature was fundamentally conflicting. On the one hand, there was the view of a gentle side of nature, including such images as helpful wood nymphs, springs and meadows, and a happy, carefree country life. On the other hand, there was that of the fearsome powers of nature – dark forests, raging streams, stormy seas and wild animals evoked fear and terror. The divine powers and demons who ruled here needed to be calmed by ritual. Agriculture meant an injury to nature, which required rites of expiation; these were also performed when cities were built. The religious respect for the environment was also expressed in the admiration for the fertility gods such as Demeter/Ceres, and the calendar of feast days, with their offerings of thanks and petition, such as the Thargelia in April/May at which the first-fruits were celebrated. Ritual offerings were also made to such climatic elements as the wind, rain and drought, to ensure good harvests.[1]

In addition to these more emotional, irrational views, however, there was also an investigation of the laws of nature. Ionian natural philosophy in the sixth century BC went beyond purely mythical thinking, and tried to explain the world rationally. Instead of holding the gods responsible for natural events, geophysical principles were explored. The doctrines of the four elements fire, air, earth and water by Empedocles of Agrigentum (*c.* 495–435 BC) and of the smallest indivisible elements, the theory of atomism proposed by Leucippus and his pupil Democritus of Abdera (460–370 BC), were important initial approaches. At the same time, a distinct environmental determinism emerged, promoted particularly by the Hippocratic school of the fifth and fourth centuries BC, and especially reflected in Hippocrates' *On Airs, Waters, and Places* (*Peri aeron, hydaton, topon*).

[1] Panessa 1991, I.499–541.

This treatise construed a connection between the condition of human
health and human environment: illness and health were dependent on
habitat. The conditions of life and political constitutions were seen as
determined by location, composition of the soil, climate, wind conditions, sunshine, quality of the water and cosmic influences. Asia, it was
argued, had a mild, balanced climate and rich vegetation, which supposedly produced soft people who were little suited to battle. Europe by
contrast had a harsh and changeable climate, which brought forth tough,
industrious people, well conditioned for warfare:

Inhabitants of a region which is mountainous, rugged, high, and watered,
where the changes of the seasons exhibit sharp contrasts, are likely to be of big
physique, with a nature well adapted for endurance and courage, and such
possess not a little wildness and ferocity. The inhabitants of hollow regions,
that are meadowy, stifling, with more hot than cool winds, and where the
water used is hot, will be neither tall nor well-made, but inclined to be broad,
fleshy, and dark-haired [i.e., the Boeotians]; they themselves are dark rather
than fair, less subject to phlegm than to bile. Similar bravery and endurance
are not by nature part of their character, but the imposition of law can produce
them artificially ... These are the most important factors that create differences in men's constitutions; next come the land in which a man is reared,
and the water. For in general you will find assimilated to the nature of the
land both the physique and the characteristics of the inhabitants. (Hippocr.
aër. 24; Loeb)

Another two basic attitudes are connected with the ambivalent relationship of people to nature as both a benign and a dangerous force: on
the one hand, a feeling of inferiority, based on the subjugation of human
beings to their environment; on the other, a sense of superiority which
presupposes human dominion over nature, and the idea that the human
being can gain control over nature. In Sophocles' *Antigone* (442 BC), the
choir speaks (332ff.):

Many wonders there be, but naught more wondrous than man:
Over the surging sea, with a whitening south wind wan,
Through the foam of the firth, man makes his perilous way;
And the eldest of deities, Earth, that knows not toil nor decay
Ever he furrows and scores, as his team, year in year out,
With breed of the yokèd horse, the ploughshare turneth about.
The light-witted birds of the air, the beasts of the weald and the wood
He traps with his woven snare, and the brood of the briny flood.
Master of cunning he: the savage bull, and the hart
Who roams the mountain free, are tamed by his infinite art;
And the shaggy rough-maned steed is broken to bear the bit.   (Loeb)

These two divergent basic attitudes had an effect too on the doctrine of the emergence of culture, which also existed in two different versions. The 'Descendancy Theory' was based on the legend of the golden age, as reflected in Hesiod's *Works and Days* (*Erga kai hemerai*), in which nature grants a paradisiacal life which, however, becomes ever more arduous, as a result of which people intrude sinfully upon nature. This corresponds to the old Near Eastern view of four eras, each less well endowed with the good things in life than its preceding period: a golden age, followed by a silver, and then a bronze age, and finally the iron age, the contemporary period, filled as it was with tribulations. The 'Ascendency Theory', on the other hand, was connected with the doctrine of the emergence of culture, as professed by Plato and Protagoras, which was rooted in a belief in progress. It taught that humankind has escaped from its pitiful original state, in which it was at the mercy of nature and its hardships. Through the development of technology, arts, morals and political community, an ordered system of cohabitation, in which justice and law prevailed, had emerged. These two contrary positions were brought closer together through an awareness of the cycles of life, to which animals and plants, too, were subject.[2]

Such a cycle is shown as early as Homer's parable of the leaves in the forest, which appear and pass away again, like the generations of people. Glaucus of Lycia, fighting on the Trojan side in the *Iliad*, addresses his opponent Diomedes, the companion of Odysseus (*Il.* 6.146–9):

Great-hearted son of Tydeus [Diomedes], why do you inquire of my lineage? Just as are the generations of leaves, such are those also of men. As for the leaves, the wind scatters some on the earth, but the luxuriant forest sprouts others when the season of spring has come; so of men one generation springs up and another passes away. (Loeb)

The two finally discover that their families are connected in friendship, and refrain from doing battle.

From today's point of view, the positive conclusion to be drawn from such attitudes would be a call for appropriate treatment of nature. Admittedly, this would not reflect the modern idea of environmental protection, but rather a wish for compliance with a divine order, and for moderation. The philosopher Heraclitus of Ephesus (*c.* 545–480 BC) wrote that, 'Wisdom consists of speaking the truth, listening to nature, and acting in accordance with her' (D/K 22 B 112 = fr. 109 M). The

---

[2] Vögler 1997, 14ff.

tragedians of the fifth century BC held the opinion that man must adhere to the place provided for him, and perform his task in the world order.

By contrast, Plato's doctrines in the fourth century BC saw intellectual being (*logos*) as superior to material being (*physis*). That brought a new dimension into play: the liberation of the soul from its inferior, material cloaking. Nature (*physis*) thereby became an expression of the incomplete and the transitory, by contrast to the eternally existing. Observation of nature served the purpose of cognition of the harmonious world order embodied in the cosmos. Natural law also implied the right of the stronger (*Gorg.* 483c–d). Humankind, by means of technology (*techne*) and culture (*nomos*), intervened in a nature created independently of it. This was explained by the 'demiurgos', who, according to the Platonic creation myth, had formed the world using the existing predefined matter, and in accordance with a primeval ideal (*Tim.* 28c, 29a).

Aristotle (384–322 BC) by contrast upheld the concept of an eternal world, of a nature constantly in the process of creation, and existing from within itself. At the same time, however, he also gave reasons for the superiority of humans over animals (*pol.* 1254b 10ff., 1256b 15ff.). Thus, he viewed a part of nature as an object of exploitation, as spoils, although humankind itself nevertheless remained a part of the natural whole. He also supported the principle of considered moderation, or the postulate of the balanced mean, from which a certain restraint in the use of natural resources could be inferred, although it did not attain the principle of protection from ruinous intervention. As can be seen in Xenophon, faith in the inexhaustibility of resources prevailed (*vect.* 1.4, 4.2ff.).

Finally, in the Hellenistic philosophy of the Stoics, nature became a rational nature, so that dispassionate, sensible life was seen as natural. Humankind, while fatefully connected to nature, could, however, through reason (*logos*; Lat. *ratio*) also find moral fulfilment. Since its intellect empowered it to shape and control the fate of plants and animals, it was possible for it to assume its role as the master of nature. Around the same time, the philosophy of Epicurus (342/1–271/0 BC) intended, by explaining physical processes, to free people from their fear of nature and death, and from superstition, so as to enable them to lead happy lives. Moreover, the Hellenistic period saw the emergence of pastoral poetry, which expressed admiration for country life, thus providing a literary counterbalance for the urban life of the expanding cities, a tradition which was to continue during the imperial Roman era, in the idyllic landscape images in the novel *Daphnis and Chloe* (2.3) by Longus, around the turn of the second to third century AD.

CHAPTER 3

Agriculture

Agriculture formed the basis of the ancient economy, and initially served the purpose of self-sufficiency. Even the prosperous were, in their own view, not merchants or shopkeepers, but farmers and landowners. The ancient *polis* was, as Max Weber described it, a 'warriors' guild', its citizen hence a soldier who equipped and provided for himself; the city did not embody a centre of production and commerce, but rather served 'consumer interests'. For the citizens, agriculture represented the primary economic sector, so that no contradiction arose between town and countryside.

Ancient agriculture demonstrated great continuity: there was neither any revolutionary technological innovation in agriculture nor any mechanisation, only some improvements in the tools and the methods of cultivation. No large-scale enterprises came into being in the area of the skilled crafts, and mass production hardly emerged at all. In terms of forms of property and means of production, there were major differences in agriculture depending on location – 'from the highly developed Egyptian channel and irrigation system to simple pasturing and hunting economies'.[1]

Even in early Greece, the most important products were cereals, grapes and olives, and beyond that legumes (field beans, lentils, peas) and fruit (pears, apples, figs). In addition, stockbreeding, primarily of sheep but also of cattle and goats, was practised, as were fishing and hunting, primarily of wild boar, deer and so on. Two-field rotation predominated, so that half the arable land lay fallow at any time, together with common pastureland. The Mediterranean climate, with high precipitation in winter and sunny summers, allowed for a wide range of crops. In early summer, field crops and fruit were harvested, followed in late summer by grapes and olives. During their fallow year, fields were repeatedly

[1] Pekáry 1979, 4.

33

ploughed with an ox-drawn plough, and fertilised with animal dung. This was in short supply, since only draught animals were kept in stables. A common pastoral practice was transhumance, in which the herds were pastured in the valleys and plains in winter, and in the nearby mountain ranges in summer (Soph. *Oid. T.* 1133ff.).

Literary sources on Greek agriculture are scarce, and often provide only indirect indications. Hesiod of Boeotia (around 700 BC) in his poem *Works and Days* describes daily work and provides us with an agricultural calendar, but no real instructions on how to go about farming; in essence, it is a moral appeal for hard work on one's own farm. He recommends one or several slaves and draught animals, and his goals are autarky, freedom from debt, and a son as an heir (*erg.* 229ff., 375); on the other hand, he warns against engaging in commerce (618ff.).

Tyrtaeus of Sparta (second half of the seventh century BC) describes the subjugation of the neighbouring Messenians, who had to surrender half their harvest to their Spartan rulers (fr. 5D). This resulted in additional economic gains for the Spartans on their farmsteads in Laconia, which, however, also led to differences in relations of ownership. Accordingly, the lyricist Alcman around the same time describes the ordinary dishes of the people in Sparta (groats, pearl barley mush with honey, mash of legumes), shortages in the spring and the delicacies enjoyed by the rich – cake, pastries, apparently also meat from the hunt – so that, overall, fluctuating food supplies must be assumed.[2]

Around 600 BC, Athens had to contend with an agricultural crisis caused in part by population growth and overpopulation. The Attic countryside was largely in the hands of noble families; free labourers and a major portion of the former small peasants had become dependent upon them as debtors or serfs, and were thus in danger of falling into debt slavery. Leased farmland apparently cost a sixth of the yield surrendered to the lord of the manor, hence the term *hektemoroi* for 'tenant'. In this situation, Solon was elected as a 'conciliator', and introduced many reform measures, including an export ban on all food products other than olive oil (Plut. *Sol.* 24.1), restrictions on the acquisition of land (Aristot. *pol.* 1266b 16), debt relief for the citizens (*seisachtheia*, 'shaking off a burden'; Aristot. *Ath. pol.* 12.4; Poll. 7.151), the abolition of debt slavery (Aristot. *Ath. pol.* 6.1, 9.1; Plut. *Sol.* 15.2, 19.4), and a reform of weights and measures. This enabled an overall free development of the citizenry, and brought economic profits to a rising stratum of merchants.

[2] Thommen 2003, 45ff.

Topographically, Greece is characterised by small-scale structures, with relatively little fertile ground between the mountains and hills. Attica had an area of approximately 2,500 sq. km (250,000 ha), and in the fifth and fourth centuries BC was home to 250,000 inhabitants, as noted, of whom some 50,000 lived in Athens. About 5.5 per cent of the cultivatable land, or 13,000 ha, was used for cereal cultivation.[3] In 329/8 BC the Attic land produced approximately 27,000 *medimnoi* of wheat (approximately 1,000 tonnes) and 340,000 *medimnoi* of barley (approximately 11,400 tonnes; *IG* II[2] 1672), enough to feed approximately 50,000 to 60,000 people.[4] In addition, at least 800,000 *medimnoi* (approximately 27,000 tonnes) of cereals were apparently imported every year during the fourth century BC, half of it from the Black Sea (Dem. 20.31ff.), with which at least another 130,000 people could be fed.[5] The prerequisite for the imports was not only the metal and money economy which arose during the sixth century BC, but also the urbanisation and empire-building process in the Aegean area. The political control of the eastern Mediterranean and the Dardanelles proved to be vital, which is why the Delian League was founded under the leadership of Athens after 480 BC, when the Hellespont and Thrace were freed from Persian domination.

Archaeological surveys in the territory of Attica have yielded insights into the structure of rural farmsteads. The owner of the so-called Princess Farm of Agrileza (Fig. 3) was a certain Timesios, who was also known as the leaseholder of some silver mines and the owner of a second holding, the Cliff Farm, about a kilometre away, around the same time; he also acquired an additional farm from a debtor. Thus, Timesios owned almost the entire Agrileza Valley, where marble was quarried and metal mined.[6] According to the investigations of H. Lohmann in the Charaka Valley, that area contained approximately 35–40 farms and a village-like settlement. The farmsteads were equipped with fortified towers, threshing places, terraces, graves and roadways. The towers served not only for defence, to guard against robbers, but also as living and storage space. A quarter of the farmsteads belonged to large-scale farmers, with approximately 25 ha each, and together accounted for 30–50 per cent of the acreage.[7] The small peasants held only approximately a quarter of the area of the large farmers. The 2,000 richest Athenians held a quarter to a third of the cultivated land, and almost half of the farmland was in the

---

[3] Garnsey 1988, 101. [4] Garnsey 1988, 99. [5] Hopper 1979, 90.
[6] Goette 1993, 167ff. [7] Lohmann 1985, 81.

Fig. 3 Princess Farm, Agrileza Valley, Attica.

possession or under the control of 10 per cent of the population.[8] Oil and honey were the main agricultural products; mining played a rather minor role.

The fact that agriculture constituted the basis for a secure way of life was shown in connection with wars, such as the Peloponnesian War between Athens and Sparta, each supported by their respective allies (431–404 BC): Thucydides, from Athens (*c.* 460–400 BC), reports that the Spartans systematically destroyed grain fields and orchards in Attica, with the intention of depriving the enemy of his source of food (Thuc. 2.79, 3.26, 6.94). However, such measures could not be successfully implemented everywhere, and hardly had any long-term effect, since the vines and olive trees were hard to destroy completely.[9] Ultimately, Athens was cut off from its allies and food suppliers in the Aegean Sea, lost much of its strength and therefore finally had to capitulate to Sparta and its allies. Nevertheless, in later wars too, agricultural resources were repeatedly wilfully destroyed (Xen. *hell.* 4.5.10, 7.1, 5.2.39; Plut. *Cleom.* 26.1).

[8] L. Foxhall, 'The Control of Attic Landscape', in Wells 1992, 157.
[9] Hanson 1998, 55ff.

CHAPTER 4

Forests and timber

The forest cover in the Mediterranean had already been subject to significant change during the centuries before the Greek settlement. Between 5000 and 3000 BC a shift occurred in south-eastern Europe (the Balkans), with cold treeless and wooded steppes and summer-green deciduous and coniferous forests being replaced by evergreen oak-woods. An investigation of the Argolis area of the Peloponnese reveals that it was covered before the Bronze Age (i.e., prior to 3500 BC) with thick deciduous forests of downy oak; in the Bronze Age (the third and second millennia BC), by sparser woods or macchia with evergreen holm oaks and pines; and starting around 900/800 BC, by olive and walnut trees.[1] In addition to the hardwood deciduous trees, such as oak and olive, there were also such evergreen bushes as myrtle and oleander, and, particularly in higher locations, pine and cypress (Fig. 4). Cypresses grew especially in Crete, and cedars in Syria and Phoenicia, where they were primarily felled for shipbuilding (Theophr. *hist. plant.* 4.1.3, 5.7.1).

In ancient Greece the forests were already a source of energy and of building materials. The available literary information refers particularly to Athens. Attica experienced a rise in population during the seventh and sixth centuries BC, which resulted in increased clearing of the wooded slopes of the nearby Aegaleus and Hymettus Mountains (Figs. 5 and 6). More remote mountains, too, such as the Parnes, Kithairon and Pentelikon ranges, were also used to obtain wood supplies. The comic dramatist Aristophanes (*c.* 445–386 BC) in his play *The Acharnians* has charcoal burners from Acharnae appear as a choir, an indication of charcoal trade from the area of the Parnes, based on oak, maple or beech. In the Kithairon Mountains, there is a pass called Dryoskephalai ('oak heads', Hdt. 9.39), which indicates an old stand of oak. Thucydides (2.75) reports that at the end of the fifth century BC

---

[1] Jahns 1992.

Fig. 4 Olive trees and forest cover near Sparta (Acropolis): view of the Taygetus Mountains with coniferous vegetation up to 1,700 m above sea level.

Fig. 5 View from the Athenian Acropolis, above the Areopagus and the Agora, to the Aegaleus Mountains.

wood was felled on Kithairon. The Pentelikon Mountains, however, were primarily noted for quarrying of marble. On the plains there were, moreover, numerous olive plantations, which were legally protected (Dem. 43.71), but probably also scattered smaller clusters of oak, fir

Fig. 6 View from the Athenian Acropolis and the Olympieion to the
Hymettus Mountains.

and elm.[2] During the Peloponnesian War the destruction carried out by
the Spartans in the Attic countryside probably rather affected the olive
and fruit trees more than the actual woodland with building timber.[3]

However, wood was not used only for purposes of domestic construction and fuel, but also since the fifth century BC in large measure for
mining and shipbuilding. The rise of Athens caused the demand for wood
to increase considerably. Olive wood was used as firewood and for tools,
but hardly for house- or shipbuilding. Wood was a scarce commodity,
and had to be imported through the ports from nearby or even far-away
areas, such as Piraeus, Eleusis, Corinth, Samos and Knidos (*IG* II[2] 1672).[4]
Especially for shipbuilding, Attica and neighbouring Euboea could meet
only a small part of the demand for wood; the bulk was imported from the
more productive forests of northern Macedonia and Thrace (Hdt. 5.23).

In 483/2 BC, in the context of the Persian Wars, a state navy was
established in Athens with some 200 ships, which would have to be
maintained and replaced in future as well. In this regard wooded
Macedonia seemed the closest and most attractive solution for timber.
Xenophon (*c.* 430–354 BC) has Jason of Pherai, the master of Thessaly
(*c.* 380–370 BC), proclaim (*hell.* 6.1.11): 'With Macedonia in our

---

[2] Meiggs 1982, 191.   [3] Nenninger 2001, 112.   [4] Meiggs 1982, 433ff.

possession, the place from which the Athenians get their timber, we shall of course be able to construct far more ships than they' (Loeb). Also important for the timber trade was the Attic colony of Amphipolis, at the mouth of the Strymon on the southern coast of Thrace. Thucydides (4.108) reports that in 424/3 BC, the town was taken by the Spartans: 'The Athenians were greatly alarmed by the capture of Amphipolis. The chief reason was that the city was useful to them for the importation of timber for ship-building' (Loeb).

In particular Theophrastus provides important information about timber for ships (*hist. plant.* 5.7.1):

Now silver-fir, fir and Syrian cedar are, generally speaking, useful for ship-building; for triremes and long ships are made of silver-fir, because of its lightness, and merchant ships of fir, because it does not decay; while some make triremes of it also because they are ill provided with silver-fir. The people of Syria and Phoenicia use Syrian cedar, since they cannot obtain much fir either; while the people of Cyprus use Aleppo pine (*pitys*), since their island provides this and it seems to be superior to their fir (*peuke*). (Loeb)

Silver fir was most highly prized, because of its light weight; it could be found primarily in Macedonia, Thrace and Italy (Theophr. *hist. plant.* 4.5.5). The rulers Dionysius I and later Hieron II of Syracuse also obtained large quantities of wood for their extensive fleets in southern Italy and Sicily (Diod. 14.42.4–5; Athen. 5.206f, 208e–f), while Antigonos Monophthalmos of Asia Minor in 315 BC plundered Lebanon for this purpose (Diod. 19.58).

Forest utilisation and clearing were among the most conspicuous interventions in nature by the Greeks. Even in archaic times, it had already become apparent that this involved problems. Homer mentions torrential rivers which swept oak trees with them (*Il.* 11.492–5). The destructive effects of forest fires were also known since the earliest times (14.396–7, 20.490–1); however, with the exception of the fire on Sphacteria in 425 BC (Thuc. 3.98, 4.29–30, 34), they rarely appear in the literary tradition. Later, the negative effects of forest clearings on the landscape are primarily discussed by Plato (427–347 BC).

In his dialogue *Critias*, Plato imaginatively contrasts the primeval Athens of 9,000 years since with the contemporary condition, and discusses the phenomenon of deforestation and soil erosion (110c–112e). Human intervention, he notes, has eroded the earth, destroyed the habitats of animals, impaired the water balance and created a barren landscape. While this reflects contemporary clearing practices, it contains no historical analysis, and at the same time reveals an unbroken admiration for the beauty and fertility of the Attic countryside. Plato is writing not as a historian but as a philosopher, particularly about the ideal state, and at the same time criticising the monumental construction policies of the time, implemented by the Athenian politician Pericles (*c.* 490–429 BC). Even if the report displays aetiological aspects and has to be interpreted with caution, it nevertheless shows an awareness of environmental problems – which, however, gives rise neither to accusations nor to demands for a different kind of behaviour. Nor did any fundamental criticism of clear-cutting arise later, since clearing of land continued to be seen as part of the progress of civilisation. Nevertheless, the forest wardens mentioned by Aristotle (*pol.* 1321b 27–30, 1331b 14–16) are an indication that state controls were considered important in forestry, and that resources should be maintained; the Cypriot kings, too, were concerned about the protection of their trees (Theophr. *hist. plant.* 5.8.1). Obviously, even then there was the opinion that for long-term survival careful use of wood resources was necessary.

As can be seen from Plato, the damage to forests and to pastureland neither led to any immediate supply crisis, nor involved complete deforestation. Later replanting shows that intervention in the vegetation was not fundamentally irreversible. While J. V. Thirgood and J. D. Hughes have still assumed extensive deforestation,[5] O. Rackham has pointed to the rapid regeneration of evergreen oak and Aleppo pine, so that these trees were not permanently destroyed.[6] Moreover, natural scientists have come to assess the question of the regional differences in the flooding of riverbanks and the siltation of river mouths due to clear-cutting. Though there was human intervention, changes in forest cover also had natural causes. In many areas the barren condition of the landscape was caused by later natural or anthropogenic human changes, or even by clear-cutting during the nineteenth century.[7] Moreover, the idea of extensive coniferous forests, especially in southern ancient Greece, is often a fallacy. Even then, macchia vegetation with pine and oak predominated (Macr. *Sat.* 7.5.9).

---

[5] Thirgood 1981; Hughes 1994, 73ff., esp. 80ff.
[6] Rackham 1990, 93–4. [7] Nenninger 2001, 202.

CHAPTER 5

Gardens

In the Near East and Egypt the most important gardens were located in the surroundings of the ruling dynasties, with the palace and the sacred site forming a unit. The so-called Hanging Gardens of Babylon of Semiramis, an Assyrian queen who lived around 800 BC, were later included among the Seven Wonders of the Ancient World. These gardens have not been identified, but probably formed a terrace structure over dome-shaped substructures, such as those built under Nebuchadnezzar II during the first half of the sixth century BC.[1] Moreover, Near Eastern rulers kept artificial animal-parks surrounded by walls, the so-called *paradeisoi*. They served for the royal hunts, which made the king, together with the god, the lord over nature, and which also recalled the Garden of Eden. Hellenistic rulers and Roman aristocrats would later be happy to continue with this tradition.

In the city states (*poleis*) which developed in Greece during the early part of the first millennium BC, the municipal centres left space for religious ceremonies and public meetings, but the residential areas had very little green space. Sacred gardens or public sacred groves were mainly located outside the actual housing areas. According to traditional belief, sacred beings dwelt in such places – be they gods, nymphs or heroes. A sacred grove (*alsos*) was generally a place in open natural surroundings with a cluster of trees, a brook, a field or a grotto. It was marked by a ritual figure and mostly enclosed by a wall, so that the designated plot was called a *temenos*. However, unlike the Near Eastern royal gardens, it remained accessible to all. Its fundamental features were its communal religious aspect and its untamed natural character, located at the transition to civilisation. Sacred groves were thus protected against uncontrolled intervention (Thuc. 3.70.4; Callim. *hymn.* 6.24–60).

---

[1] J.-C. Margueron, 'Die Gärten im Vorderen Orient', in Carroll-Spillecke 1998, 74ff.

Fig. 7 Kerameikos cemetery in Athens.

In Athens the sacred olive trees dedicated to Athena were generally protected from being felled or dug up (Lys. 7).

Moreover, private vegetable and fruit gardens (*kepoi* and *orchatoi*) are attested for the Greek *poleis* at an early date. Homer (*Od.* 7.112ff.) describes a garden surrounded by hedges for the palace of Alcinous, the ruler of Phaeacia, where everything flourished and there was no want; it included an orchard with apples, pears, figs and olives, a vineyard and a vegetable garden, so that it was designed and irrigated without decorative plants or flowers, purely for utility (*Od.* 7.129). Laertes too, the father of Odysseus, lived in seclusion and cared for his garden, where fruit and olive trees, grapes and vegetables grew (*Od.* 24.244ff., 340ff.). In the reality of the urban residential areas of the *poleis*, house gardens were relatively rare. Greek houses had a courtyard or a peristyle (arcade) without gardens. Gardens were often located at the city walls, or formed a green belt around the city, near the rivers.[2] Here too were the garden-like graveyards, such as the Kerameikos in Athens (Fig. 7). The profession of gardener is attested as early as the fifth century BC (Athen.

---

[2] Carroll-Spillecke 1989, 40ff.; 1998, 157ff.

9.372b–c; Theophr. *hist. plant.* 7.5.2). In this context Theophrastus lists a broad range of garden vegetables and seasoning plants.[3]

In the Athens of the late classical and Hellenistic periods, new 'philosophers' gardens' were created, which provided a landscaping enrichment of the city's surroundings. These included Plato's Academy, Aristotle's Lyceum and Epicurus' Kepos – which can be translated as 'garden'. Theophrastus, a pupil of Aristotle's, had a garden near the Lyceum; his works include a comprehensive botanical study (*De causis plantarum*; Diog. Laert. 5.46, 51ff.). These 'gardens of learning' were in private hands, and could, in connection with older public institutions, provide a philosophical and athletic education. They included an assemblage of parks, shrines and sports facilities, and such buildings as gymnasia and palaestras (courts for wrestling matches) as training areas, together with pathways, statues and sacred groves, such as for the Heros Akademos, or shrines such as for Apollo Lykeios. Theophrastus' Lyceum also had an altar for the Muses.

In Hellenistic times the newly founded cities included many more park-like green spaces and groves, such as the Daphne in Antioch or the garden of the Museion in Alexandria (Strab. 17.1.8–10). The Paradeisos too was taken over by Hellenistic rulers, after Alexander the Great conquered the Near East from 334 BC and placed it under Macedonian rule (Plut. *Demetr.* 50). Also famous were the palace gardens established not only in Alexandria, but also in Syracuse under Hieron II. The urban dwellers thus not only experienced new splendour: they also were presented with nature in a new form, in a world of increasing urbanisation.

---

[3] Osborne 1992, 385.

CHAPTER 6

Animals

Animals – cattle, goats, pigs, deer, sheep, poultry, birds, fish – were a part of the food supply in antiquity, but also provided other raw materials such as wool, leather and fur. Horses, mules, oxen, elephants and camels also served as means of transport and conveyance, particularly in war. Animals were thus the companions, servants and guardians of people, and at the same time a means of entertainment and prestige in spectacles and at the hunt. Finally, they were used as sacrificial offerings to the gods, whose will was divined by observation of birds – the Roman auspices – or by the reading of entrails.

Animal husbandry was the foundation of rural subsistence. In early Greece, the stock of animals was initially a greater determinant of wealth than landholding.[1] Cattle were of the greatest economic importance, both as draught animals and as suppliers of meat and leather. Sheep, which were also held in large numbers, provided milk and wool. Together with cereals, the meat of sheep, goats and pigs formed the foundation of the diet. Dogs served as protectors and companions, particularly on the hunt; the close relationship between them and their masters is often shown expressively on grave steles.

The Greeks appear to have had two different basic attitudes in their relationship with animals. On the one hand, animals were admired as an incarnation of nature; on the other, they were seen as a hostile threat, as a natural danger to be overcome. However, animals also had a role as mediators between gods and humans, for example in ritual sacrifices; their fat and entrails were burned on the altars, and their meat eaten. Animals were regarded as permanent companions and interpreters of the gods, and could also have symbolic significance, as expressed in the constellations of the zodiac, and in their association with certain gods.

---

[1] Richter 1968, 32ff.

In the Near East many gods had been venerated in animal form. Animals, particularly the deer, bull, panther and lion, at the same time also represented attributes of the gods. In Egypt there were animal divinities such as the royal god Amun (in the form of a ram), the fertility god Apis (in the form of a bull), and the fertility goddesses Hathor/Isis (in the form of a cow). Gods were often represented with human bodies and animal heads: thus the seated goddess Sachmet ('the most powerful') of Memphis has a lion's head, expressing her unbridled nature and her unpredictability. Here animals were already seen as mediators between humans and gods. There was a partnership between them, since both derived from the creator god, so that only he could be the master of the animals. Dead animals were treated like the human deceased; they entered as Osiris into the nature of the god, and thus obtained religious protection.[2]

In the Old Testament, on the other hand, the representation of the divine in animal form is rejected. In Exodus 32 the golden calf created by Aaron is venerated by the Israelites, whereupon they are punished. There is a clear separation between the human and the animal; moreover, there is a division between pure and impure animals. Blood may not be ingested, since the soul lives in it. The animal is nevertheless regarded as a creature of God, the one closest to the human being.

In Greece the gods took anthropomorphic form; nevertheless they also had the goat-legged Pan, or Poseidon's son Triton, with a snake's or horse's body. Animals functioned as attributes of the gods: the eagle was assigned to Zeus, the owl to Athena, the ram to Hermes, dogs and snakes to Asclepius. Animals were thus representatives, projections, of divine power. Artemis was seen as the mistress and protector of animals (*potnia theron*) and of the hunt. In the Greek legends gods turned themselves or other people into animals: Zeus turns into a swan or a bull; Actaeon is turned into a stag by Aphrodite and torn to pieces by his dogs.

Moreover, we encounter numerous beings of mixed nature: centaurs, sirens, griffins, gorgons (Medusa), phoenixes and sphinxes; the fire-breathing Chimaera, with her lion's head, the goat's head on her back and her snake's tail, combines the hostile powers of three animals. In the legends such dangerous monsters in wild nature are overcome by heroes: Heracles conquers the Nemean lion, and Theseus the Minotaur. The coat of the slain lion becomes Heracles' trophy, and lends him strength. The lion symbolises bravery, ferocity and power; as a stone guardian on graves,

---

[2] Hornung 1967; Prieur 1988, 33ff.

it has apotropaic power, the ability to ward off evil. In real life it was exterminated in Greece, along with the leopard and the hyena, by the dawn of the Christian era.[3]

Images of animals appear in Greece earlier than human images. Small bronze horses go back to the tenth century BC, their cylindrical bodies and broad legs emphasising the speed of their legs. The horse, which was already in use during the Mycenaean era (sixteenth to eleventh centuries BC), was an object of prestige, and embodied wealth and status. It could be used in battle and for hunting. Chariot teams served both for war and for sport. Deer and birds appear from the eighth century BC; thereafter, there are images of animal fights. The ram served as a guardian and symbolised both aggressiveness and resistance at the same time.

Animals such as the lion, boar, bull and wolf, as well as bees and birds, appear in parables as early as Homer, and are known from fables since the sixth century BC – primarily Aesop's – complete with the human traits ascribed to them: the stubborn donkey, the sly fox, the cowardly rabbit, the faithful and bold dog, the courageous lion, the stupid sheep, the insidious snake, the dirty pig, the dangerous wolf: they are the standards for human behaviour and ethical orientation. In comedies such as Aristophanes' *Frogs, Wasps* or *Birds*, animal choirs appear, and create a critical distance from the human community.

Zoology, as the science of animals, was not established until Aristotle in the fourth century BC (*part. an.* 645a 6). He lists over 550 species of animals, distinguishing those 'with blood' from those 'without blood'. However, since animals were without reason (*logos*) or faith, people were not required to deal justly with them. By propagating human superiority over animals, Aristotle made the latter an object of exploitation (*pol.* 1254b 10ff., 1256b 15ff.). The Stoics in the third century BC derived a natural law under which animals were mere creatures of instinct, which they demonstrated by their behaviour. Animals were irrational and created for humans, who, thanks to their *logos*, had the right to dispose of them (Sen. *epist.* 76.9–10).

Nevertheless, there was already at an early stage criticism of anthropocentrism, which assumed that animals were by nature superior to humans. Animal protection and vegetarianism reached back at least to the Pythagoreans, who believed in the transmigration of souls and wanted to avoid shedding blood (Ov. *met.* 15.463–9). Aristotle's pupil Theophrastus in the fourth century BC called for the protection of animals for ethical reasons,

[3] Hughes 1994, 105–6.

and criticised blood sacrifices (Porphyr. *abst.* 2.5ff., 20ff.). However, the majority assumption was that humans had no moral obligation towards animals, which justified interventions in animal populations, and would later influence Rome and also Christianity.

CHAPTER 7

Food

BASIC FOODS

Food and diet provide an obvious direct reference to the environment and nature in antiquity. Food had long been associated with human well-being, and this was reflected in the medical literature. The *Corpus Hippocraticum*, a collection of medical texts from the fifth to the third centuries BC, contains a document about diet which particularly describes a right lifestyle and also addresses the question of food and knowing what is beneficial for humans:

> These things therefore the author must know, and further the power possessed severally by all the foods and drinks of our regimen, both the power each of them possessed by nature and the power given them by the constraint of human art ... And it is necessary, as it appears, to discern the power of the various exercises, both natural exercises and artificial, to know which of them tends to increase flesh and which to lessen it; and not only this, but also to proportion exercise to bulk of food, to the constitution of the patient, to the age of the individual, to the season of the year, to the changes of the winds, to the situation of the region in which the patient resides, and to the constitution of the year ... If indeed in addition to these things it were possible to discover for the constitution of each individual a due proportion of food to exercise, with no inaccuracy either of excess or of defect, an exact discovery of health for men would have been made. (Hippocr. *vict.* 1.2; Loeb)

With regard to food supply in ancient times, the ancient historian P. Garnsey distinguishes between 'food crises', which he considers to be endemic, and 'famines', which he sees as having appeared only occasion-ally.[1] Moreover, he explains that in cases of food shortages and emergen-cies, chronic malnutrition or insufficient diet must be assumed. The assumption that the state of health of the population was generally good

---

[1] Garnsey 1999.

in Graeco-Roman times is thus called into question. Garnsey accordingly points to illnesses caused by an inadequate diet or vitamin deficiency, such as bladder stones, eye complaints and rickets.[2] One should also note the 'famine food' mentioned by the Roman doctor Galen (AD 129–c. 216), which could replace or 'stretch' the food supply in bad times.[3] Children and women were particularly affected by poor diet; overall, the urban population was disadvantaged compared with the rural population.

Why

In Greece the community meal of the men had a long tradition, and was tied into a ritualistic framework. Unlike in Rome, women were excluded from it. The meal (*deipnon*) had a preparatory ritual nature; the ensuing drinking session (*symposion*) was the central element. As a rule, private homes were equipped with a dining room (*andron*), where one could recline on *klinai/clinae*. This is shown particularly well by the so-called row or standard houses in Piraeus, or in Colophon and Olynthus. The best known *symposion* is presumably the one described by Plato in his dialogue of that name; it was reportedly held in 416 BC in the house of the Athenian tragedian Agathon, to celebrate his victory in a tragedy competition. Here, eulogies were held to Eros, and prior resolutions to the contrary notwithstanding, large quantities of wine drunk. Socrates was the only one to come through the effort with no sleep, and got back to his day's work again at dawn.

Prior to a *symposion*, the hosts would write down the names of the participants, with the date and time, on little wax panels, which were distributed to the guests by a slave. The beginning of the feast was at the ninth hour, and the number of participants limited to approximately nine guests; women were excluded, other than hetaerae, who were permitted to provide entertainment. Nevertheless, a special moral canon prevailed, supervised by a *symposiarchos*, often a guest selected by lot; it contained regulations regarding the mixing of the wine, the sizes of the vessels, the type of entertainment and so on. The *symposion* began after the meal had been cleared away. First, flower tendrils were distributed, a libation was offered, a hymn to the gods was sung; then, the drinking session was opened and wine was served.[4] There might then be more small servings of food or dessert: cakes and pastries, honey, nuts, cheese and fruits.

The basic foods in Greece, besides wine, were cereals and olive oil. In Attica, while olive trees were plentiful, cereals were hardly sufficient. Since the soil was light and not very thick, barley, which is only half as nourishing as wheat, was the main crop. As mentioned above in

---

[2] Garnsey 1999, 45ff.   [3] Garnsey 1999, 36ff.   [4] Garland 1998, 95ff.

connection with agriculture, this shortage of the latter always made imports, primarily from the Black Sea area, necessary. Thanks to Athenian control of the Aegean, this precarious self-sufficiency could, in classical times, largely be compensated, and numerous goods, such as salted fish, imported or exchanged for oil and honey.

Plutarch (*c.* AD 45–before 125), albeit writing later, in Roman imperial times, provides information about the diet in Sparta (*Lyc.* 12). Since it is based on a report from around 300 BC (Athen. 4.141c), it can also be used, with caution, for Sparta in earlier days:

> They met in companies of fifteen, a few more or less, and each one of the mess-mates contributed monthly a bushel (*medimnos*) of barley-meal, eight *choai* of wine, five minas of cheese, two and a half pounds of figs, and in addition to this, a very small sum of money for relishes (*opson*). Besides this, whenever anyone made a sacrifice of first-fruits, or brought home game from the hunt, he sent a portion to his mess (*syssition*). For whenever anyone was belated by a sacrifice or the chase, he was allowed to sup at home, but the rest had to be at the mess. (Loeb, modified by author)

A bushel yields approximately 74.5 litres of flour (or 68 kg of bread); eight measures of wine correspond to approximately 37.2 litres, and five minas of cheese to approximately 3 kg. That works out at almost 2.5 litres of barley and 1.25 litres of wine per day – a generous daily total of well over 6,000 kcal, but we know nothing about its allocation. At all events, cereals appear here too to have been the basic foodstuff, while meat was seen as a rarity, and there is no mention of the notorious blood soup. Self-sufficiency, which was maintained even after the loss of the lands in Messenia in 369 BC, remained a central principle.[5]

THE SYMBOLISM OF FOOD: BEANS AND FISH

In addition to the social aspect, the symbolic content of food and food taboos must also be taken into account; the bean and the fish are particularly important in this respect. The most important bean species in antiquity was the small-seeded broad bean (*vicia faba*), also known as the horse or field bean. It was frequently prepared as mash, but also used in salads, vegetable dishes and stews. The bean was easily storable, was nourishing and provided a supplement to cereals. Since it was rich in protein, it later also became an important food for gladiators. Finally, as a substitute for meat, it was a meal for poorer people.

[5] Thommen 2003, 130–1.

Symbolically, the bean had both positive and negative aspects. It was nutritious, but also had a destructive aspect, since it caused flatulence, diarrhoea, stomach cramps, sleeplessness, confusion and attacks of weakness, and was in some cases fatal. Bean poison could lead to favism, a blood disease (haemolytic anaemia). In the area of religious symbolism, the bean embodied the antithesis to the spices which represented the food of the gods and symbolised the golden age.[6]

For this reason, the bean also appears as a food taboo. The Orphics and the Pythagoreans placed a ban on the bean which the Neopythagoreans continued in Hellenistic and Roman times. At celebrations of the corn goddess Demeter, too, beans were forbidden (Paus. 8.15.3). The Orphics believed in the transmigration of the soul; intermittently, they believed, it was in Hades, and had to pass through a cycle of reincarnations in order to achieve its ultimate liberation from the human body. To this end, it was necessary to observe ascetic rules, particularly the renunciation of meat and the ban on beans. The philosopher Pythagoras promulgated the teaching of the transmigration of the soul at the end of the sixth century BC; he developed the concept of the soul into a dogma.

From this point of view, the bean served as a support and ladder for souls when they returned from Hades to the light of the day; the 'knotless' stem symbolised the transition from the lower to the upper world, and created the connection between the world of the dead in Hades and the world of the living (D/K 58 C 3 = fr. 99 M). The real reason for the ban on beans was that the bean was equated with meat, which was also banned. Since the Pythagoreans considered the bean a phenomenon of flesh and blood, compliance with the food taboo was indispensable for reincarnation. However, as vegetarians, the Pythagoreans constituted an exception in antiquity, and had no broad impact. The image of the bean had little effect on its consumption. Prescriptive regulations existed only in a narrow circle of philosophers, or in special religious associations. For these vegetarians, eating meat and performing blood sacrifice were tantamount to murder.

The fish was also seen as a dualistic, strongly contradictory creature. Owing to its negative connotations, it was to some extent treated with disgust, and its consumption banned. The Pythagoreans had a ban on the consumption of goatfish (Diog. Laert. 8.33–4). Nevertheless, fish was relatively frequently eaten, though not necessarily as the main food. For people in ancient times, it was difficult to classify anatomically. According

[6] Garnsey 1998.

to Anaximander of Miletus (*c.* 610–545 BC), living beings had arisen from the dampness, the human being, however, in a fish – a smooth shark, since he required lengthy care (D/K 12 A 11, 30 = fr. 28, 26 M). The fact that certain fish could also eat people was threatening. The fish came from the sea, a dangerous anti-world which could turn upon people. Moreover, the sea was regarded as poor, since wealth came from the land – from agriculture. The fisherman was the classic image of a life in poverty: he did not occupy himself with the usual crops, but hunted and gathered – and a kilo of fish contains only two-thirds of the calories of a kilo of cereals.[7]

However, the fish was also regarded as a symbol of fortune, as the return of the ring thrown into the sea by Polycrates of Samos indicates (Hdt. 3.41ff.). The fisherman was therefore a symbol of dependence on fortune, which was tied to the sea. A real preference for fish only developed in the upper classes. In Roman times aristocrats installed fish-ponds (*piscinae/vivaria*) on their estates, and cared for the fish; this became a symbol for an exquisite lifestyle. Anthony and Cleopatra too went fishing (Plut. *Ant.* 29). A villa with a view of the water, with fisherfolk, was highly valued. Thus, fish was on the one hand indispensable, particularly in times of scarce resources; on the other, it was a symbol of abundance and cultivation.

Ultimately, too, the fish became a symbol for Jesus Christ, the Greek word for fish, *ichthys*, being an acronym for *Iesous Christos Theou Hyios Soter* ('Jesus Christ, son of God, saviour'). Galilean fishermen were to become 'fishers of men' (Matthew 4.19; Mark 1.16–17); baptism was seen as such a 'fishing expedition' – as the rescue of believers from the sea of this world. The sharing of fish obtained Eucharistic significance: at Holy Communion, fish, like bread, was a symbol for the body of Christ.

[7] Purcell 1995.

CHAPTER 8

Fire and water

MYTHOLOGY

The ancient legends explained earthly and celestial phenomena and conditions, and thus provided help in orientation and existence. Accordingly, explanatory models also existed for fire and for ritualistic dealings with sacrificial fire. In Greek mythology, Prometheus was considered the bearer of fire. He came from the old family of gods, the Titans, who harked back to Uranus (the sky) and Gaia (the earth), which had then succumbed in the battle with the Olympian gods under Zeus. Prometheus was a symbol of uprising and rebellion, a champion of humankind against the hostility of the gods. The 'forward-thinking one', as his name can be translated, became the creator of the human race, and its saviour in the form of the bearing of fire. He was also seen as the god of craftsmen and inventor of all arts.[1]

After Prometheus had created the human race from clay, Zeus wanted to destroy the fragile humans and create new ones. Zeus tried to starve the people by demanding the best parts of their food as sacrifice. Prometheus then cut an ox into pieces, separating the edible and the non-edible parts, the meat from the bones. He disguised the two parts and tried to fool Zeus into choosing the bones. Zeus saw through the trick and planned revenge. He left the meat to the people, while the gods settled for the smoke of the burned bones as a sacrifice. Thus, people need meat, they get hungry and are therefore dependent, transitory – ultimately, mortal, while the gods are independent, undemanding and immortal. The legend explains and justifies the sacrifice as the separation of the people from the gods, a separation which is, however, overcome by that very sacrifice.

Since Zeus in his wrath wanted to withhold fire from people, Prometheus secretly brought it down to earth by carrying charcoal in a giant fennel from

---

[1] Böhme and Böhme 1996, 64ff.

Mount Olympus, where he had taken it from the sky or sun chariot – or, according to a different version, from the smithy of Hephaestus, the god of fire. Thus did people obtain artificial fire, which had to be maintained continually – unlike the lightning bolts with which Zeus intruded upon the world's affairs. Fire distinguished people from the animals, since without it they too would have had to eat meat raw. Moreover, it created ties to the gods, although the people had also to accept the superiority of the gods.

Zeus was furious, and had the immortal Prometheus caught and chained to a cliff near the Okeanos. Zeus' eagle fed daily on his liver. In the legend salvation finally appeared: Heracles killed the eagle and relieved Prometheus. The gods took cruel revenge on the people for this: Zeus ordered Hephaestus to create the first woman, Pandora, 'the all-endowed', and gave her a small box containing every evil. When she descended to earth and opened it, the sufferings and sins escaped to grip hold of humankind (Hes. *theog.* 571ff.; *erg.* 6off.).

Parallel to the mythical explanation, fire had also been ritualistically venerated since ancient times in the form of Hestia, the goddess of the fireplace and the family hearth and domesticity. As the inventor of the building of houses, she protected those seeking shelter in any building, and brought personal safety and fortune; her fire was sacred. The domestic hearth was a centre and place of worship of the family; at the same time, it was an altar with a charcoal fire where an offering could be made before each meal. There was also a state hearth in the council building of the city, the *prytaneion*. Hestia was Zeus' sister, and was the only Olympian divinity who was never involved in war or strife, hence she was the mildest, most charitable and most just of the gods and goddesses of Olympus. She remained a virgin under an oath to Zeus, and demanded the same of her priestesses, so as to fulfil the ideal of purity and overcoming of the material. Hence the negative aspect of the destructive or of a purgatory was lacking, so that death by fire could be seen as liberating, and cremation as justified. Despite its dangerous effects, fire was generally seen as a centre of the community and as a cleansing bearer of culture.

On the other hand, the sun was not among the phenomena ritualistically venerated by the Greeks; there was no sun worship. Instead, the concept of Helios – initially a being not worshiped – as the driver of the chariot of fire prevailed. Only in the course of time did he attain an important position as the driver who moved and directed, and only in the Hellenistic period, starting in the third century BC, did a Helios cult arise.

Water too was, like fire, a life-giving and cleansing element included in ritual ceremonies. The Okeanos, the world ocean, embodied one of the primeval forces from which the gods had arisen. The sea gods Poseidon and Amphitrite were ritualistically venerated by the Greeks. Waters and springs were generally associated with such divine beings as river gods and nymphs, to whom shrines and festivals were dedicated. The nymphs included the Nereids, or sea nymphs, and the naiades at the springs. In addition, however, there was the dangerous Styx, the river to the under-world. According to the myth, the great flood had once blotted out almost all life, but Deucalion had survived, and had made a new development possible, which had led to civilisation. This myth thus provided explan-ations for cyclical phenomena and processes of change in nature. How-ever, no specific protection for the waters was ever derived from this.

SCIENCE: THE FOUR ELEMENTS

In addition to mythology, the Greeks also developed natural science and philosophy, which sought rational explanations for natural phenomena. They developed the doctrine of the four elements earth, air, fire and water, of which, they believed, the entire earth consisted. They saw water, fire and air as the primal matter from which all things developed. The sun too was, in the view of Empedocles of Agrigentum (*c.* 495–435 BC), a powerful ball of fire (D/K 31 A 49 = fr. 43 M). Around the same time, Anaxagoras of Clazomenae (*c.* 500–428 BC) claimed that the sun was a glowing rock (D/K 59 A 42 = fr. 48 M).

According to Anaximander (*c.* 610–545 BC), who considered the uni-versal substance to be the Indefinite (*apeiron*), living beings had arisen from the primal dampness (D/K 12 A 30 = fr. 26 M). In Empedocles' view the four elements earth, air, fire and water were eternal, and appeared in various mixtures or aggregates; the earth had, he believed, brought forth single body parts, such as heads, arms and eyes, from the water and fire, after which these had united to form human bodies (D/K 31 B 57, 62 = fr. 89, 95 M). In medical discourse, too, the four elements began to play a central role in connection with the four bodily fluids, or 'humours', blood, yellow bile, black bile and phlegm. A disturbance of the balance between these basic elements would, according to Hippocrates, cause illness in the body (*nat. hom.* 1.1, 4.1–3). If the heat formed by the fire in the blood became too great, the blood would disintegrate and cause water to be excreted in the form of sweat; if it were reduced, sleep would follow; if it were extinguished entirely, the result would be coldness and death (Hippocr. *morb. sacr.* 7.13–14; *flat.* 14.2). Thus did natural-scientific explanation arise, juxtaposed with the myth according to which Prometheus had formed the first human out of clay, and Athena breathed life into him.

While the Okeanos was, in Homer (*Il.* 18.607–8), still a river flowing ring-like around the flat earth, later concepts saw the sea as carrying the land masses and permeating all waters. Thales of Miletus (*c.* 625–545 BC), whom Aristotle saw as the 'father of philosophy', was the first to try to explain the world rationally; he saw water as the very basis of all things. In his view, the world had developed from an original state in which there was only water; the earth too was now a plate floating upon it (D/K 11 A 12 = fr. 10 M). Along with Plato's concept of an underground water cycle, the model of an atmospheric water cycle, as proposed by Xenophanes, Empedocles and Anaxagoras, established itself. In his meteorology Aristotle developed the theory of evaporation, condensation and cloud formation. Water was thus not only the primal element, but also constituted the prerequisite for all life. Since there was a chronic water shortage in southern Europe, even in antiquity, it was already necessary from an early stage to channel and supply water artificially.

HYDRAULIC ENGINEERING AND WATER POISONING

Major achievements in the supply of water can be attributed to the ancient Greeks. Generally, drinking water was obtained from spring catch-works and wells (*krenai*), which were fed both by groundwater and by water brought in artificially. For the supply of a city, moreover, cisterns were indispensable (Aristot. *pol.* 1330b 5ff.). Water brought in by aqueduct and rainwater were stored in both private and public cisterns.

Fresh-water mains and sewage ditches can be found in Greek cities even in archaic times. In the second half of the sixth century BC, a real breakthrough was achieved in hydraulic engineering. Samos built a 2 km long aqueduct into its municipal area, which ran through a tunnel 1 km long (the Eupalinos Tunnel). Athens had an archaic network of clay pipes, connected to a fountain house on the Agora.[2] Themistocles, who attained fame primarily as a politician and military commander during the Persian Wars, also served as the supervisor of the aqueducts at the beginning of the fifth century BC (Plut. *Them.* 31).

---

[2] Tölle-Kastenbein 1994.

Moreover, around 400 BC, pressurised water lines of clay pipes appeared, as the example of Olynthus demonstrates. Another technical innovation appeared in Pergamum in later times, where high-pressure water mains were installed in the second century BC to supply the mountain fortress; still later, in Roman times, this system was supplemented by aqueducts. Here, the clay pipes had a diameter of 16–20 cm, and consisted of several segments, each up to 42 km long. Special officials (*astynomoi*) took care that the cisterns were properly maintained, and that the town-dwellers kept the streets adjacent to their houses clean (*SEG* XIII 521 = *OGIS* 483).[3]

Pollution was nonetheless an issue in the cities; in Athens, the Eridanos River was ultimately badly polluted (Strab. 9.1.19). In Hellenistic times, too, river poisoning seems to have been a problem: at all events, a mass poisoning of Nile water is recorded, with many casualties (Athen. 2.42a). Thucydides (2.48.2) notes reports of hostile well-poisoning in Athens during the Peloponnesian War; later, the Athenians would themselves attempt to destroy the water pipes of besieged Syracuse (6.100.1).

Under the Macedonian king Alexander the Great a technical intervention in the water balance of Boeotia was undertaken, in which the outflows of Lake Copaïs were dredged, so that the level of the lake dropped, and an unwelcome marshland was reclaimed for agriculture (Strab. 9.2.18). Here, older efforts at drainage, such as those carried out in Arcadia in the Peloponnese, provided a precedent (Thuc. 5.65.4). In Larisa in Thessaly a lake was drained, which led to a cooling-off of the climate in this area (Theophr. *caus. plant.* 5.14.2–3). In many other areas, however, aridity and drought were a recurring problem; nonetheless, the dams and dykes built in ancient Greece for water management served neither for extensive irrigation nor for water supply, and were only used again on a large scale by the Romans.[4]

---

[3] Klaffenbach 1954; G. Garbrecht, 'Die Wasserversorgung des antiken Pergamon', in Frontinus-Gesellschaft 1991, 19ff.
[4] Tölle-Kastenbein 1990, 115ff.; Krasilnikoff 2002.

CHAPTER 9

Earthquakes and volcanoes

EARTHQUAKES

The area we are examining lies along the Mediterranean/Trans-Asian earthquake belt, and is thus exposed to a high degree of seismicity. Tectonic movements and fracture cleavages caused frequent earthquakes in antiquity. These included both subsidence earthquakes, caused by the collapse of underground caverns, and volcanic and tectonic earthquakes; mudslides and tsunamis were also classed as earthquakes.[1] Both the actions of the gods and natural processes put forward by Ionic natural philosophy were called upon to provide explanations for these phenomena. In the mythological tradition, Poseidon, described as the 'earth-shaker' (Ennosigaios), was primarily held responsible for earthquakes. It was therefore necessary to avoid provoking such supernatural powers to fits of anger.

In the scientific view, three interpretations of the earthquake phenomenon arose, the 'Neptunic', the 'pneumatic' and the 'volcanic', along with various combinations of these. In the sixth century BC, Thales of Miletus saw the earth as a kind of ship on an ocean, the waves of which caused it to tremble (Sen. *nat.* 3.14.1). Anaximander and Anaximenes thought that earthquakes were triggered by air in the fissures of the earth, while Anaxagoras saw seismic shocks as the result of streams of air which had penetrated the earth (Sen. *nat.* 6.10.1; Amm. Marc. 17.7.12). In classical times Democritus broached the 'Neptunic' view that the cause of earthquakes was water currents in underground caverns which had penetrated under the flat earth's surface (Aristot. *meteor.* 365b), while Empedocles (D/K 31 A 68–9) and Antiphon (D/K 87 B 30–1) supported the 'volcanic' theory, which claimed that seismic shocks were caused by fires within the earth. Finally, a new version of the pneumatic approach, propagated by

---

[1] Waldherr 1997, 35ff.

Aristotle in the fourth century BC, gained influence: it posited a porous earth filled with penetrated air (*pneuma*), the pressure of which increased as a result of water seeping in, so that it pressed outward (Aristot. *meteor.* 365a–369a). Like Antiphon (*c.* 480–411 BC), the scholar Posidonius (*c.* 135–51 BC) saw a connection between seismic and volcanic activities, and thought that fire and water were seeking a way to escape through underground passages. Posidonius also divided the earth into endangered and safe areas (cf. Strab. 12.8.17–18).

The historian and geographer Demetrius of Callatis (*c.* 200 BC) and later Demetrius of Scepsis (*c.* 200–130 BC) were the first to compile listings of earthquakes (Strab. 1.3.17, 20). The best known and most serious cases of reported earthquakes involved Sparta in 464 BC (Thuc. 1.101, 128) and Helike/Bura in 373 BC, before which the animals had allegedly fled (Aristot. *meteor.* 343b, 344b, 368b; Ael. *nat. anim.* 11.19). The earthquake in Sparta caused massive destruction of the municipal area, and cost 20,000 lives, according to Diodorus (11.63); it was interpreted as divine retribution for a sin committed against enslaved helots whose refuge was the shrine of Poseidon on Tainaron (Thuc. 1.128). Thucydides also reported a submarine earthquake with a tsunami in 426 BC (3.89) in the Atalanti channel near Euboea (cf. Strab. 1.3.20). Then, in 227 BC, an earthquake in Rhodes gave cause for relief actions by Hellenistic rulers (Polyb. 5.88–90). However, only in Roman times do we have knowledge of any real precautionary measures.

VOLCANOES

Volcanic phenomena were seen in Graeco-Roman antiquity as the work of underground forces locked in prison caves beneath the volcanoes. After the Cyclops and the Hecatonchires (the 'hundred-armed' ones) had been held captive in the interior of the earth, the Titans too, the children of Uranus and Gaia, were also locked up in Tartaros after their defeat by the Olympian gods (Hes. *theog.* 139ff.). In the myths, however, Hephaestus or Vulcan, too, had his fires here, which would repeatedly come to the surface. The Cyclops were also involved, supposedly as smith's apprentices to whom the volcanic activities of Mount Etna or the Liparian islands were attributed (Callim. *hymn.* 3.46–7), as was Typhon, another monster locked up by Zeus (Pind. *Ol.* 4.6). The giants, Gaia's sons from the blood of Uranus, were also associated with Vesuvius, since they had been defeated on the Phlegraean Fields near the Gulf of Pozzuoli, west of

Naples (see Fig. 20 below), by Heracles in their battle against the gods of Mount Olympus, and banished beneath the earth (Diod. 4.21.5ff.).

In the fifth century BC, volcanism was associated with earthquakes, that is, they were both attributed to the same causes, with Aristotle thereafter in good measure responsible for this breakthrough, which was achieved by his pneumatic theory (*meteor.* 365b). Mount Etna had broken out repeatedly during the fifth and fourth centuries BC, which Greek authors did not fail to note – particularly the eruptions of 479 BC (Aesch. *Prom.* 367–8; Pind. *Pyth.* 1.20ff.), 425 BC (Thuc. 3.116) and 396 BC (Diod. 14.59.3). Empedocles was reported to have climbed into the mountain's crater to explore it, and allegedly even fell in (Strab. 6.2.8); moreover, an underground connection with the volcano of the Liparian islands was suspected (Diod. 5.7.4). Finally, with regard to Etna, Posidonius praised the advantages of lava and volcanic soil (Strab. 6.2.3), which was preferred for viniculture. There were, however, no more true volcanic catastrophes in the Greek world after the Thera/Santorini eruption in the middle of the second millennium BC.

CHAPTER 10

Mining

Ancient society had a high demand not only for wood, but also for rock and clay for construction, and for metals, which were used for all sorts of purposes in the trades and in artistic work. Clay and rock were quarried at the surface; the quarries were as a rule in the near vicinity of the cities. The best known marble quarries were in the Pentelikon Mountains near Athens, on the Cycladic islands of Paros and Naxos, and in the Peloponnese. Moreover, gold, silver, tin, copper, lead and iron were mined in various places, often in subterranean mines. Owing to the scarcity of resources and the high procurement costs, quite a number of materials and products were repeatedly reused throughout antiquity (Hdt. 3.6).

Metals had been mined in Greece, Asia Minor, Dacia and Spain since the Neolithic era, with copper and tin, for which Britain was famous, the most important products (Strab. 4.5.2; Diod. 5.22.1ff., 38.4–5; Tac. *Agr.* 12.6).[1] Since the third millennium BC, bronze had been produced as an alloy of copper and tin, and Cyprus early developed into a leading centre for copper mining. Silver was mined in large quantities on the Aegean island of Siphnos (Hdt. 3.57–8; Paus. 10.11.2), as was gold on the island of Thasos, where the entire Mount Scapte Hyle was supposedly deforested and dug up (Hdt. 6.46–7).

Lead and silver had been mined in Laureion, the mining area in southern Attica, since the Mycenaean period (Fig. 8). At the beginning of the fifth century BC, subterranean mining was initiated, with over 2,000 shafts up to 50 m deep or more, and with lateral galleries up to 40 m long.[2] Washeries (Figs. 9 and 10) and smelting furnaces, too, were built, which polluted the air and water considerably. The air was contaminated

---

[1] Penhallurick 1986, 115ff.   [2] Schneider 1992, 76.

Fig. 8 Ancient mining area in the Souriza Valley, Laureion, Attica.

by sulphur dioxide and lead vapours, which led to extensive physical health impairments, such as infertility and genetic damage, nerve diseases and anaemia.[3] The workers, for the most part slaves, could number between 10,000 and 30,000, and were always exposed to the danger of being buried in a cave-in. Moreover, large numbers of trees had to be felled in the immediate and even the more remote surrounding forests, which led to soil erosion and a drop in the groundwater level. These drawbacks were accepted, however. In the first century BC the geographer Strabo still considered mines a generally beneficial measure against dense, uncultivated forests (Strab. 14.6.5).

All in all, mining, with its associated polluting activities, caused one of the most serious impacts on the landscape, even if its extent may seem limited in comparison with the total area involved. It left huge heaps of slag and overburden, and damage to the stripped surfaces and the effects of subsidence are visible to this day. The Romans continued this activity in various areas on a large scale (Diod. 5.35–6), and thus once again added greatly to the level of environmental damage.

[3] Healy 1978, 133ff.; Domergue 2008, 45ff.

Fig. 9 Ancient cistern and washery in the Souriza Valley, Laureion, Attica.

Fig. 10 Ancient washery in Thorikos, Attica.

PART II

Rome

CHAPTER II

The geographic space

ROME AND ITALY

The origin of the Roman Empire was its capital, Rome, where a cluster of several little hilltop settlements joined together to form an urban centre during the eighth and seventh centuries BC, and then gradually incorporated the surrounding countryside of Latium. Rome was located at a key point in central Italy, on the lower Tiber, approximately 25 km from the coast. It was situated not only at a major river crossing, but also at a trade junction where the Salt Road (via Salaria) running from the coast to the Sabine hinterland crossed the north–south route between Etruria and Campania. Accordingly, a trade forum developed early on the banks of the Tiber: the cattle market (forum Boarium), where fragments of Greek vessels are among the finds dating back to the eighth century BC. In addition, a central meeting square, the forum Romanum, was built for the emerging community of citizens at the foot of the Capitol, where the main municipal shrine, to the god Jupiter, was located (see Fig. 22 below).

After the expanding city was put to the torch by the Gallic Celts in 387 BC, an 11 km long fortified wall, the so-called Servian Wall, was built around it a few years later. This encompassed an area of 426 ha, which became ever more densely populated over time. Since the city had grown organically, it had no rectangular street grid; the roads to the countryside emerged from Rome like rays. After the food merchants had been expelled from the forum Romanum in the late fourth century BC, the square in the third and second centuries BC changed further into a political and administrative centre, with prestigious temples and basilicas. By the early and middle republican period, the city had developed into the leading economic and political nodal point in central Italy, although at that time it had only a river port, for the seaport of Ostia would not be built until the middle of the first century AD, under Emperor Claudius.

Rome's geographical position held both opportunities and perils. Despite its central location, the city was also peripheral to both the Etruscan and Latin areas. Rome, with its initially modest surrounding countryside, was a city state in Latium dominated by noble families, and was constantly forced to defend itself against mountain tribes seeking new settlement lands on the coast. In this struggle, however, Rome itself displayed expansionist tendencies, and took over neighbouring territories. By 400 BC the nearby Etruscan city of Veii had been conquered and incorporated into Roman territory – the beginning of a continuous expansion of the city's domain which was to bring access to the resources of the wooded Apennines and the fertile fields and pastures of central and southern Italy. By 270 BC all of Italy south of the Po was subject to Rome. Expansion beyond Italy was now only a matter of time.

By the end of the republican period, Rome had grown into a metropolis of some one million inhabitants, for whom a considerable infrastructure was provided. However, the Romans not only developed many new settlement areas, but also became acquainted with the numerous problems of a major city – traffic, noise, and the stench of waste and of open fires. These problems also started to appear at numerous other places in the empire.

THE ROMAN EMPIRE

Roman expansion led to a massive transformation of the Mediterranean area by the first century BC. The Roman conquest of Italy was followed by the expansion to Sicily and then to other areas of the western and eastern Mediterranean, where Roman provinces were set up in succession: Sicily, Sardinia and Corsica in 227 BC, Spain in 197 BC, Macedonia and Greece (Achaea) in 148–146 BC, Asia (Minor) in 129 BC and Egypt in 30 BC. In 15 BC the first Roman emperor, Augustus (27 BC to AD 14), launched the Alpine campaign, the beginning of the conquest of northern Europe, in which Rome pushed its boundaries to the Rhine and the Danube. In the east the Euphrates was the boundary, so that the empire embraced a gigantic territory of over 50 million inhabitants. Further advances beyond these rivers, as well as to Britain, were yet to follow.

In his *Geschichte der Landschaft in Mitteleuropa*, Hansjörg Küster in 1995 pointed to the extensive changes which took place in southern central Europe as a result of its incorporation into the Roman Empire. For the first time the agricultural areas and resources of the area north of the Alps were intensively utilised. South-central Europe was clearly bounded by the Rhine and Danube, and within this area the essential features of a uniform culture could develop. Here were settled a large. number of people – how many is unknown – who knew how to farm the land with new methods. Urban settlements, ports, road networks and manors with intensive animal husbandry, farming, orchards and pastures arose. Vineyards and wheat farms were introduced to the area, and figs, spices and oil were imported from the south. The forests of the north were used for the first time on a large scale for timber construction. In Germany, which Tacitus described as a country of fearsome forests and dismal swamps (*Germ.* 5.1), the Romans had access only to a small portion of the country.

The land was developed through road-building, parcelled out by 'limitation' (surveying and construction of boundary paths crossing at right angles), and allocated or leased to Roman citizens. The spectrum of the settlements ranged from existing native towns raised to *municipia*, through newly established Roman citizen cities (*coloniae*) and little settlements on key transport routes (*vici*/villages), to manors (*villae*) scattered throughout the country. Cities were often built on the slopes above rivers or at the confluence of two or more rivers – Coblenz and Passau in Germany, or Augst and Windisch in Switzerland – while the villas tended to be built in neighbouring loess areas (Fig. 11).

Despite the intensive land use and forest clearing in Roman times, the ancient impacts generally took place in relatively modest dimensions and were in some cases compensated by new tree planting or by reafforestation. As we will see, in the Main–Danube area of Württemberg, for example, sediments caused by increased flooding can be ascertained for the first to the third centuries AD, with oak logs embedded in it; only in post-Roman times did new floodplain forests grow back. The imperial spatial development, with its dense road network, which has to some extent survived into modern times, also had long-term effects.

THE ROMAN ROADS

Roads provide information not only about political, military and economic contexts, but also about the manner in which a society overcomes distance and controls its space. In the Near East the Assyrians already had an extensive road network in the eighth and seventh centuries BC, which was later expanded still further by the Persians (Achaemenids), for whom it served the administrative and military consolidation of their huge empire. Unlike the Greeks, the Etruscans at an early stage already had

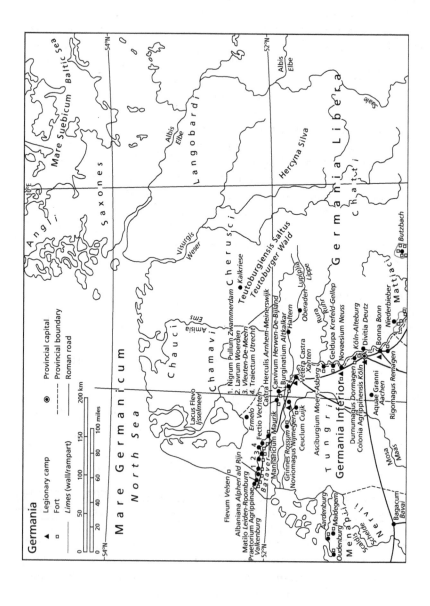

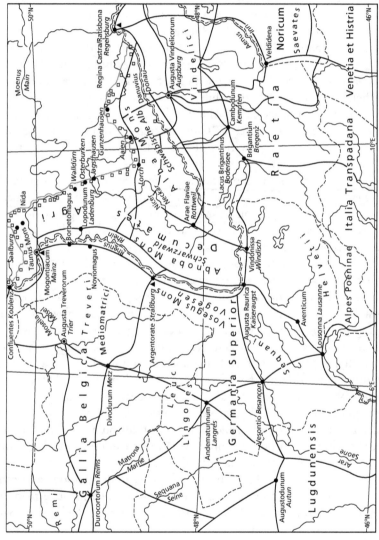

Fig. 11 Roman Germany: settlements, the road network, the Rhine boundary and the *limes*.

city streets and roads in Italy. Marzabotto near Bologna had a right-angled street grid in the fifth century BC, with drainage trenches on both sides.[1]

Starting with the construction of the via Appia in 312 BC, the Romans gradually developed a far-flung road network, with an ultimate length of 80,000 to 100,000 km, running throughout their realm. Starting in 15 BC, the Alpine area too was tied into the road network. The route across the Little St Bernard Pass connected the Aosta Valley in north-western Italy with Lugdunum (Lyon) in the Rhone Valley, while the road over the Great St Bernard linked that area to Lake Geneva and Augusta Raurica (Augst near Basel) in the upper Rhine area of northern Switzerland. The via Claudia Augusta led over the Reschen Pass from Bozen/Bolzano in northern Italy to Augsburg, while a parallel route crossed the Brenner Pass. Another route across the Alps ran from Augsburg via Kempten and Bregenz on Lake Constance to Chur in eastern Switzerland, and from there across any of several Grisons passes, such as the San Bernardino, to northern Italy (Fig. 11).

The roads served the army for troop movements and resupply, the merchants and traders for the transport of goods, and the imperial administration for the rapid dispatch of messengers. Augustus founded the *cursus publicus*, a state courier and transport system which included the provision of official trips at public expense. Local people were required to make state messengers, transport carts and draught animals available, for which they were, however, compensated.[2]

The roads were mostly built by army troops and ran as straight as possible, or else along old routes or mule tracks. The goal was to avoid having to build such structures as arched bridges, tunnels, causeways or cliff-retention supports, which were expensive and time-consuming. Generally, roads were not built in valley bottoms, which were prone to flooding, but rather on the sides of valleys or along ridges. Paved streets existed largely in the cities and near settlements, but country roads too were sometimes paved. The more common gravel roads could be built faster and repaired more easily. They were built on a reinforced under-layer and lined with border-stones. Milestones (*miliaria*), roadside stone columns 2 to 4 m high, marked the distances.[3]

Typical travellers included business people, traders, troops and other army people, magistrates, couriers of the *cursus publicus*, statesmen and even the emperor himself. Private persons took trips to the baths at Baiae

---

[1] Schneider 1982, 4ff.; Giebel 2000, 35–6, 131–2.   [2] Kolb 2000, 123ff.
[3] Schneider 1982, 29ff., 102ff.; Bender 1989, 115ff.

on the Gulf of Naples, made educational journeys to the philosophers' schools in Greece – Cicero visited Athens, and Julius Caesar, Rhodes – and visited shrines such as Delphi and Olympia, and natural scenic sites such as the Tempe Valley in Thessaly or the grotto at Parnassus. Egypt was the destination of dreams.[4] Even if mass tourism did not yet exist in antiquity, a critique of tourism already did – from the philosophers. On the one hand, journeys were seen as healthy hardships which made the traveller tough – a beneficial restriction to simple food and lodging, which strengthened body and soul – on the other, criticism was directed at extreme luxury of travel and ceaseless restlessness (Sen. *epist.* 87.2ff., 104.13ff.; *tranq.* 2.13ff.).

Journeys were taken on foot – for the rich, that meant in a litter – in the saddle, usually on a donkey or mule, rarely on a horse, or by wagon. Overnight accommodation was provided by inns (*mansiones*), and changing stations (*mutationes*) exchanged draught animals and repaired vehicles. In land transport, oxen and horses, donkeys and mules were used as beasts of burden or harnessed to draw two- and four-wheeled wagons.[5] Bulk goods and heavy loads were transported by water, on the rivers or by sea. The extensive transport network which made possible the exchange of goods over long distances led both to the import of new products and to the specialisation of traditional production centres and agricultural landscapes. Roman roads were in any case in use until well into the Middle Ages, and have been repeatedly repaired and in some cases used to this day. They thus contributed significantly to the development and integration of western Europe.

---

[4] Casson 1974, 229ff., 257ff.; Giebel 2000, 197ff.   [5] Bender 1989, 142ff.

CHAPTER 12

People and nature

The Roman calendar was filled with feast days associated with the divinity of nature and her gifts: the Fordicidia for the earth mother Tellus, the Cerialia for the corn goddess Ceres, and the Vinalia for Jupiter and Venus. Moreover, in springtime, the Ambarvalia was held for Dea Dia, the goddess of farming, and the Ludi Florales for Flora, the goddess of plants; in the autumn, the Vertumnalia for Vertumnus and Pomona celebrated the seasonal blessing of fruit. As a peasant people close to nature, the Romans saw the trees, woods and crops as gifts of the gods, but they also knew how to exploit nature and subjugate it. The cultivation of the countryside by clearing, parcelling and road-building was cele-brated as a victory over wild nature. During the Augustan period, the poets Vergil and Propertius praised the superior strength of the Roman Empire precisely because of its better environment. Augustus himself propagated the concept of world domination, according to which the Romans were viewed as an element of divine providence. The world was pacified by the Pax Augusta, and in Rome between 13 and 9 BC the Peace Altar was built; there the nurturing Mother Earth (Tellus) was displayed alongside the god-fearing imperial family.

Generally, the Romans could, like the Greeks before them, adopt either of two different attitudes towards nature (*natura*, the translation of the Greek *physis*). Roman literature on the one hand reveals pessimism, in the form of the idea of an accursed nature, which would one day succumb and disintegrate with the universe. According to the poet Lucretius (*c.* 96–55 BC), humankind was abusing its skills and knowledge, and was unable to check its desires, so that despite its superiority it was rushing headlong to disaster (Lucr. 2.1154ff., 5.195ff., 1430ff.). But literature also propagated optimism, for humankind was seen as the creator, and thus had the right to dispose of nature, which it had subjugated (Cic. *nat. deor.* 2.152):

and we alone have the power of controlling the most violent of nature's offspring, the sea and the winds, thanks to the science of navigation, and we use and enjoy many products of the sea. Likewise the entire command of the commodities produced on land is vested in humankind. We enjoy the fruits of the plains and of the mountains, the rivers and the lakes are ours, we sow corn, we plant trees, we fertilise the soil by irrigation, we confine the rivers and straighten or divert their courses. In fine, by means of our hands we essay to create as it were a second world within the world of nature. (Loeb)

Ultimately, the world and nature could not exist without the power of a ruler (*imperium*) (Cic. *leg.* 3.3).

Characteristic of the conflicting relationship to nature is Vergil (70–19 BC) in his *Georgics*, a poem about farming. Vergil not only celebrates economic profit, but also animals and plants, and he respects the divine in nature. He nevertheless assigns a leading role to humankind, since, with its intellect, it is able to maintain the natural order. Statius (*c.* AD 40–96) puts it even more clearly in his poem about the country house of a certain Pollio Felix at Surrentum:

Here are spots that Nature has favoured, here she has been outdone and given way to the settler and learnt gentleness in ways unknown before. Here, where you now see level ground, was hill; the halls you enter were wild country; where now tall groves appear, there was once not even soil: its owner has tamed the place, and as he shaped and conquered the rocks, the earth gladly gave way before him. See how the cliff learns to bear the yoke, how the dwellings force their entry and the mountain is bidden withdraw. (*silv.* 2.2.52–9; Loeb)

This view of tamed nature was expressed in a preference for open groves over dark forests, gentle hills over wild mountains, and calm waters and shorelines over rough seas. Thus does Livy (21.58.3) speak of the *foeditas Alpium*, the ugliness of the Alps.[1]

Individual Romans might criticise such ecologically harmful behaviour as destructive mining, clear-cutting of mountain forests, the extermination of plants, or the building of large manors and rural villas, which blocked the lakesides; rarely, however, were countermeasures taken, for material advantages had priority. As we will see below with regard to agriculture, the literature on the topic – Cato, Varro, Columella – reveals no love of nature, but rather an interest in utility and profit. Protection of nature was only important if preservation of resources – with a view toward future profit – was a factor.

[1] Thüry 1993, 558.

On the other hand, voices of caution did emerge from philosophical circles. After the historian Sallust (86–34 BC) denounced the destructive luxury of the upper class (*Catil.* 13), Seneca (*c.* AD 4–65) during the early imperial period imparted Stoic moderation and criticised excesses of luxury as an offence against nature: 'If we follow Nature, all is easy and unobstructed; but if we combat Nature, our life differs not a whit from that of men who row against the current' (*epist.* 122.19; Loeb). Here, too, however, it is not protection of nature, but rather fitting in sensibly with the existing world order, with the goal of moral fortification, that is the point. Natural processes, such as disastrous floods, were seen as following a definite plan, so that humans might hardly influence them.

The fundamental dilemma of people in antiquity with respect to nature can ultimately be seen in the officer and historian Pliny the Elder (AD 23/4– 79): the human, according to Pliny, has a weak constitution, threatened by nature and the environment. He leads a merciless struggle for existence which he might survive only with the aid of his technical resources. At the same time, however, he destroys his own basic living conditions, as demonstrated particularly by the example of mining. The mining of mineral resources, Pliny believed, had ultimately brought nothing but misfortune to humankind (Plin. *nat.* 2.158–9, 33.1–6).

CHAPTER 13

Agriculture

The Romans saw themselves as a peasant people, and were proud of their rural origins. Agricultural literature, which flourished from the second century BC to the first century AD, and which propagated ties to the soil, was at the same time aimed at increasing production and profit. Agriculture was not only the basis of livelihood, but also of wealth, which was primarily manifested in landholding (Plin. *epist.* 3.19, 6.19).

Economic interests were also a factor in the expansion of the Roman Empire, which began to take over the entire Mediterranean region after the middle of the third century BC. Rome profited from the taxes of the provinces, and took over their landscapes, first by land surveying and parcelling, then also by intensified construction. North Africa supplied olives and cereals; Spain, wine and oil; Sicily and Egypt, cereals – the latter probably yielding two harvests a year. Under Augustus, 20 million *modii* – approximately 150,000 tons – of cereals were delivered to Rome each year (Aur. Vict. *epit. Caes.* 1.6). Despite these imports, however, scarcities were never impossible in the capital, so that Italic agriculture continued to be of great importance, despite a number of setbacks.[1]

Agriculture in Italy was very diverse. Farmed fields with crop rotation predominated (Varr. *rust.* 1.44.1–2; Verg. *georg.* 1.73ff.; Plin. *nat.* 18.49ff.); to some extent, the Romans had already initiated the later three-field system, although two-field rotation was still the most common method. A year of cultivation would hence be followed by a year lying fallow, during which time the field could be used by cattle for pasture. Various cereals and types of vegetable could be grown alternately. Use of fertiliser made more regular use possible, so that fallow years could be avoided. Animal dung, compost and ash were the available fertilisers (Varr. *rust.* 1.38.1ff.; Plin. *nat.* 17.42ff., 18.192ff.). According to Columella (2.1.1ff.) in the first century AD, soils should not age if fertilisers were used. If no

---

[1] Lepelley 1998, 36ff., 52ff.

fertiliser was used, half the fields were left unfarmed every other year, and had to be ploughed fairly often during this time (Verg. *georg.* 1.71–2; Colum. 2.9.15; Plin. *nat.* 18.176–7). Vergil, who recommended crop rotation and the use of fallow fields and of fertilisers, also mentioned burning off fields. At the same time, he connected human dominion over the earth, which he conveyed, with a respect for the divine (*georg.* 1.96ff.). The fact that overexploitation led to leaching out of the soils – the quality of which could be distinguished – had been recognised in principle (Colum. 1 *praef.* 1ff.).

Agriculture first of all served to provide the personal subsistence of the peasants, who moreover also depended on sales in the nearest town (Cat. *agr.* 7.1; Varr. *rust.* 1.16.3) or on exports further afield. Viniculture was the most profitable type of farming. Olives were also productive, and less work-intensive than cereals. Besides that, fruit and vegetables were raised, and bee-keeping and silviculture pursued; the woods could also be used for pig raising (Varr. *rust.* 2.4.20).[2] The main animals were sheep, poultry and cattle. Goats too were common, but in the immediate surroundings of farmsteads they could destroy gardens and kill young trees (Verg. *georg.* 2.196; Plin. *nat.* 8.204). Nevertheless, animal husbandry was described as generally the most lucrative rural pursuit (Varr. *rust.* 2.1.11). In addition to pasturing, there were also various forms of transhumance, which had become established primarily in southern Italy since the second century BC. Varro kept his cattle herds in the Reatine Mountains in summer, and in Apulia in winter (Varr. *rust.* 2.2.9). Such migratory grazing practices remained common into late antiquity, but were never dominant.[3]

During the Second Punic War (218–201 BC) large areas of southern Italy had been devastated. These were then confiscated as Roman state land (*ager publicus*), and allocated for farming. At the same time the Roman conquests of the second century BC meant an increased burden for the peasants and citizens, who had to absent themselves from their fields for overseas wars for long periods of time. Moreover, cheap cereals from the overseas provinces increasingly came onto the market. This made reorientation towards wine and olive production necessary, and also to pasturing, all of which required greater expense and effort, although that did not generally diminish the areas used for cereal cultivation.[4] At the same time, the emergence of large estates was favoured; these were able to turn forest and grazing areas into farmland in areas distant from the coasts.

[2] Nenninger 2001, 41–2.   [3] Flach 1990, 146, 303.   [4] Jongmann 2003.

In this situation the tribunes Tiberius and Gaius Gracchus (in office 133 and 123/2 BC, respectively) proposed a reapportionment of the state land (*ager publicus*), according to which needy peasants were apparently to receive farms (Plut. *Tib. Gracch.* 8; App. *civ.* 1.7ff.) of up to 30 *iugera* (8 ha) (*CIL* I² 585, line 14). Although this was only a low average size, implementation of the land reform was largely blocked by the ruling classes.[5] Vineyards and olive groves of 100–500 *iugera* spread in Latium and Campania.[6] An ideal estate would be approximately 200–300 *iugera* (50–80 ha) in size, while the ever larger estates could cover as much as 90 sq. km; Pliny the Younger (AD 61/2–c. 114) was said to have owned a total of 35,000 *iugera*.[7]

M. Porcius Cato (234–149 BC), who wrote a work called *On Agriculture*, considered an estate with its accompanying buildings, equipment, plantations, cattle and staff as the greatest of possessions. A farmer should never buy rashly, and always consider all factors (*agr. praef.* 1.1ff.). His goal should be to pass on to his descendants more purchased than inherited land (Colum. 1 *praef.* 7, 10). The management of the estate was essentially carried out as follows. For his estate in Campania, which consisted of a number of separate parts, Cato had various administrators to whom he issued instructions. The operation was oriented towards the market and the money economy, and employed both craftsmen and day labourers. The estate contained various acreages: first, an olive plantation of 240 acres (*c.* 60 ha) with 5,000 trees, which yielded 30,000 bushels of olives, with an administrator (*vilicus*) and 11 slaves; second, a wine-growing estate of 100 acres (25 ha), with wine- and olive presses, as well as a granary with a threshing floor, run by another administrator and 16 slaves; between these facilities lay fertilised land with fodder grasses, where sheep and draught oxen were held between the harvest and the sowing, as well as in winter; third, there were the fields of cereals, cultivated by tenants; fourth, there was pastureland with grass and oak-woods, which was used for pasturing the herds of others in winter, part of which was located on state land.[8]

In Italy there were different basic types of estates (*villae rusticae*), with a residential house around which stables, lofts, storehouses and workshops were grouped. Often, the residential and work buildings were arranged around three sides of a peristyle court.[9] Columella, writing about agricultural operations in the first century AD, distinguished between the manor

---

[5] Molthagen 1973.   [6] Dohr 1965, 151–2.   [7] White 1970, 406; Pekáry 1979, 88.
[8] Gummerus 1906, 15ff.; Schönberger 1980, 402–3.   [9] Flach 1990, 215ff.

house (*villa urbana*), the work area with the farm labourers' house (*villa rustica*), and the storage area, with crop storerooms (*fructuaria*). He recommended halfway up a hill as the site of the farmstead; villages had been built at such locations since the Neolithic period:

> But as the nature of the farm and the method of its cultivation is a matter of importance, even so is the construction of the farmstead and the convenience of its arrangement . . . As to the qualities of a building site, I shall now speak in general terms. As a building which is begun should be situated in a healthful region, so too in the most healthful part of the region . . . Let there be sought, then, an atmosphere free from excesses of heat and cold; this is usually maintained halfway up a hill, because, not being in a hollow, it is not numbed with winter's frosts or baked with steaming heat in summer, and, not being perched on the top of a mountain, it is not fretted at every season of the year with every little breeze or rain. The best situation, then, is halfway up a slope, but on a little eminence, so that when a torrent formed by the rains at the summit pours around it the foundations will not be torn away. (Colum. 1.4.6ff.; Loeb)

However, the term *villa rustica* also described the actual farming operation in a comprehensive sense. This form of operation was commonly
adopted in the provinces, so that it also appeared north of the Alps. Here,
we encounter villas modelled after the Italic *villae urbanae*, but embody-
ing a whole class of buildings outside the townships, located in the midst
of the farmland. They had an enclosed courtyard area with a work section
(*pars rustica*), run by an administrator (*vilicus*) and separated by a wall
from the manor (*pars urbana*): see Fig. 12. Such a complex represented a
whole economic and production centre, which, along with staff quarters
and stables, also included workshops (brickworks, pottery, iron smelting).
The villas themselves were in a Mediterranean style, patterned after the
Italic *villae urbanae*. They often had a raised, richly furnished and elong-
ated manor house with a columned hall in front and corner risalites
(projecting building sections). Moreover, the heatable dwelling was
equipped with bathing facilities, terraces, gardens and decorative water
basins.

Cereal cultivation (wheat, spelt, barley) was central for agriculture in
the provinces; it was accompanied by the growing of fruit and vegetables
and by cattle pasturing. For the northern and eastern provinces, cattle
were the predominant domesticated animals, and were accordingly bred
further. In many areas of the empire, exogenous animals and plants were
also introduced. In addition to the very common grapes and wheat,
vegetables such as celery and red beets appeared in many places, as did

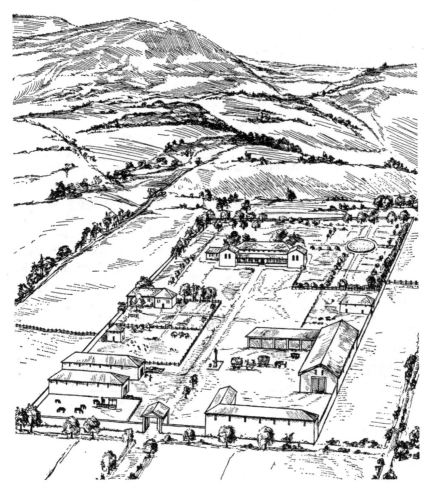

Fig. 12 Reconstruction drawing of a *villa rustica* in south-western Germany.

orchards with apples, pears, cherries, plums and nuts – as has been ascertained in various areas, such as Switzerland and England.[10]

The acreages were considerable, and amounted to approximately 50–100 ha, or even 200 ha in the case of one villa in south-western Germany.[11] Since a team of oxen could plough only approximately 0.25 ha (1 *iugerum*: Plin. *nat.* 18.9) a day, considerable investment in cattle had to be made. The villas were accordingly often located at the transition

---

[10] Flutsch et al. 2002, 34; cf. Chapter 22, n. 7, below.   [11] Drexhage et al. 2002, 75.

between damp pastures or remnants of forests in the lowlands and the dry fields in the hills. Much wood was needed for the rural operations and their maintenance, which was obtained by clearing the surrounding oak forests. Valuable humus was washed from the cleared grounds into the river valleys, which resulted in increased flooding and the creation of new damp meadows.[12] The villas thus contributed significantly to the change in the landscape.

Towards the end of the third century AD, the sizes of large-scale farms increased in the Roman Empire once again. Large estates were managed mainly by leasing to small farmers (*coloni*). Thus, the colonate was increasingly transformed into a permanent, hereditary leasehold. These ties to the land served on the one hand to guarantee the tenants economic security and thus to avoid flight from the land. On the other, their purpose was to guarantee regular tax yields. Moreover, the *coloni* were often more profitable than slaves, whose numbers declined. At the same time, the institution of the *patrocinium* was increasingly common: for protection against tax agents, peasants turned to influential officials or landlords, who in return collected rents in cash or in kind. Peasants sometimes also surrendered their land to large landowners to escape from debts or taxes.[13] Nevertheless, both free small peasant holdings and the slave economy remained in place to late antiquity. Owing to a labour shortage, however, fields were increasingly neglected and settlements abandoned, so that they were in many cases reconquered by nature.

[12] Kuhnen and Riemer 1994, 79ff.   [13] Pekáry 1979, 127–8.

CHAPTER 14

Forests and timber

The relationship of the Romans to the forest reflected their basic view of nature. On the one hand, the forest was a dark and dismal place, the haunt of wild animals and the questionable gods who held sway there (Plin. *nat.* 12.3; Sen. *epist.* 4.41.3). Silvanus, Pan/Faunus and the fauns reduced people to terror with their weird voices. The Romans often used adjectives such as *ferus* (wild), *foedus* (horrible), *horridus, obscurus* or *occultus* to describe the forests.[1] The historian Tacitus (*c.* AD 55–120) described Germany as a country of terrible forests and dismal swamps (*Germ.* 5.1). The forests were seen as the primeval starting point of human life (Vitr. 2.1.1), and as the habitat of barbarians who were at a low stage of civilisation (Lucr. 5.948ff.). The forests were moreover a strategic challenge, particularly in Gaul, Germany and Britain, since the enemy there could withdraw into them and lay ambushes, as was done in the battle of Teutoburg Forest in AD 9. Hence, military advances into these areas necessarily involved the massive felling of trees (Caes. *Gall.* 3.28–9; Lucan. 3.394ff.).

On the other hand, the forest was a piece of nature's beauty (*locus amoenus*), a pleasant place to linger under shady trees. This could involve the public forest (*silva*), a protected grove (*lucus*) or, in particular, a private piece of woodland belonging to an estate (*nemus*). Here the forest might serve for relaxation and conversation during the hunt (Hor. *epist.* 1.4.4–5; Plin. *epist.* 1.6.2, 2.8.1, 5.6.7–8).

Pliny the Elder writes in his natural history (12.1–5):

The riches of earth's bounty were for a long time hidden, and the trees and forests were supposed to be the supreme gift bestowed by her on man. These first provided him with food, their foliage carpeted his cave and their bark served him for raiment; there are still races which practise this mode of life. This inspires us

---

[1] Nenninger 2001, 30–1.

with ever greater and greater wonder that starting from these beginnings man has come to quarry the mountains for marbles, to go as far as China for raiment, and to explore the depths of the Red Sea for the pearl and the bowels of the earth for the emerald ... Once upon a time trees were the temples of the deities, and in conformity with primitive ritual, simple country places even now dedicate a tree of exceptional height to a god; nor do we pay greater worship to images shining with gold and ivory than to the forests and to the very silences that they contain. The different kinds of trees are kept perpetually dedicated to their own divinities, for instance, the chestnut-oak to Jove, the bay to Apollo, the olive to Minerva, the myrtle to Venus, the poplar to Hercules; nay, more, we also believe that the Silvani and Fauns and various kinds of goddesses are, as it were, assigned to the forests from heaven, and as their own special divinities ... We use a tree to furrow the seas and to bring the lands nearer together, we use a tree for building houses. (Loeb)

Like Pliny (*nat.* 31.53), other authors too recognised that clear-cutting could lead to flooding. Vergil (*georg.* 1.481–3; *Aen.* 2.305–7) and Lucan (2.409–10) mention the raging Po and write of farmland washed away; Horace speaks of uprooted trees (*carm.* 3.29.33–41), and Ovid, of torrential brooks which threaten farmsteads (*met.* 8.552–5); Lucretius mentions forest fires caused by clearing, hunting, warfare and lightning (5.1241ff.) – though he describes it as progress when wild forests and groves in higher locations give way to cultivated trees (5.1370ff.). The geographer Strabo too (*c.* 64/3 BC to AD 23/6) still considered clearings to be an achievement of civilisation, along with mining (14.6.5).

Even if no further-reaching measures for the protection of forests are apparent here, wood was not simply freely available. Certain forests were indeed protected, because of various property rights and strategic considerations, for example in Macedonia (Liv. 45.29.14) and in Lebanon (*CIL* III 180; *IGLSyr* 5056, 5070, 5086). Moreover, reafforestation was already being carried out at an early date – for economic reasons (Theophr. *hist. plant.* 2.2.2ff.; Varr. *rust.* 1.6.5), to safeguard precious wood resources and economically valuable space in particular areas. Finally, the forests were an essential element of agriculture, and served as forest pastures; oak-woods in particular were used for pig raising (Varr. *rust.* 2.4.20). Moreover, the trees were the main source of wood (Plin. *nat.* 16.62) for construction and fuel, and for shipbuilding.

Although much wood for shipbuilding was available in Italy and Corsica (Theophr. *hist. plant.* 4.5.5, 5.8.13), timber, including pine, cypress and cedar from the Black Sea area and the Caucasus, had been imported since the late republican period (Verg. *georg.* 2.440–5; Hor. *carm.* 1.14.11–12). When Rome built its first navy during the First Punic War (264–241 BC), oaks and firs were transported on the Tiber from Etruria, Umbria and Latium for this purpose. The extensive recently conquered Sila Forest in Bruttium in Lucania (modern Basilicata in southern Italy) also provided much wood for shipbuilding and house construction (Dion. Hal. 20.15). The Romans also transported tree trunks by river to Rome from the thickly wooded area of Tyrrhenia in Etruria (Strab. 5.2.5).

The timber industry of course made clearing necessary, which in some places both impaired the appearance of the landscape and changed the soil. In the area around Rome, the deposited sediments increased tenfold as a result of new farmland being opened up in the second century BC.[2] As mentioned above, increased sediment deposits in the river beds near the Gulf of Taranto in Lucania have been ascertained for the Graeco-Roman period.[3] This intensified land and forest utilisation was ultimately also apparent in the provinces.

In Germany, forest cover consisted for the most part of mixed oak and beech deciduous forests, which were felled periodically throughout the period from 600 BC to AD 400. At Auerberg Mountain near Bernbeuren in the Allgäu region of southern Germany, it has been shown that in certain areas the Romans specifically felled firs,[4] which were otherwise found largely in areas outside the *limes* (Fig. 11); apparently this political boundary generally coincided with the natural boundary between deciduous and coniferous forests.[5] Württemberg in south-western Germany provides a particularly evident example of how clearing and forest pasturing over-exploited the forests.

Using the growth rings of trees, it is possible to determine when they were felled. Such dendrochronological dating of floodplain oaks uprooted by the raging water and embedded in river gravel documents increased flooding for the Main–Danube area during the period from the first to the third centuries AD; it declined again during the fourth and fifth centuries. Tree pollen was reduced considerably by comparison with non-tree pollen (from grasses and herbs), which shows that forest areas had been reduced by comparison with cultivated areas. Oaks and firs could not regenerate fast enough, because of their long growth periods. The result was a thinning of the forests, and a general reduction in their area. This accelerated the surface run-off of the water, so that the topsoil of the fields was washed away and deposited in the river valleys as floodplain loam sediment. Flood beds and damp biotopes spread in the valleys.

[2] Judson 1968.   [3] Brückner 1986; cf. Chapter 1, n. 11, above.   [4] Küster 1994.
[5] Nenninger 2001, 102–3, 204.

(a)

(b)

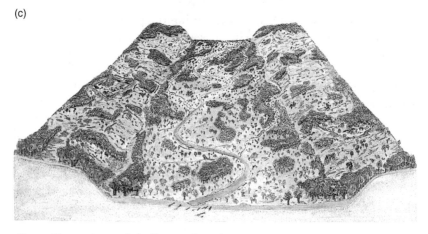

(c)

Fig. 13 Changes in wooded valley meadows due to Roman settlement in south-western Germany (pre-Roman times; Roman period; era of the Great Migration).

River courses shifted and valley floors were widened. Hillside sites, which were preferred for *villae rusticae*, were abandoned to erosion and achieved lower yields. However, with the decline in the Roman settlement in the fourth century AD, new floodplain forests grew back, and flooding became less common. The forest was able to recover despite the overexploitation, but the appearance of the landscape had changed inasmuch as the oaks had largely disappeared (Fig. 13).[6]

---

[6] B. Becker, 'Raubbau am Wald', in Kuhnen 1992, 36ff., 71ff.

CHAPTER 15

Gardens

The Romans had gardens in various forms, both in the cities and in the countryside. They are known to us primarily from Pompeii and Herculaneum near Naples, the cities destroyed in AD 79 by the eruption of Mount Vesuvius, where the volcanic material covered and preserved extensive finds. In Rome itself they are attested for the middle of the fifth century BC, inasmuch as the Law of the Twelve Tables made provision for the boundaries of neighbouring properties (Tab. 7.2): an olive or fig tree might be planted no nearer than 9 feet from the property line, and other trees no nearer than 5 feet (cf. Tab. 7.9a/b and 10; Plin. *nat.* 16.15). The garden formed a central economic base so that, at that time, a farmstead near Rome was not yet called a *villa*, but rather a *hortus* (garden) (Plin. *nat.* 19.50).

The kitchen and vegetable garden was the oldest form of Roman garden. It is attested since the fourth and third centuries BC, and was widespread in Pompeii up to the second century BC. In private homes one passed through the *tablinum* (picture room) of the atrium into a small vegetable garden (*hortus*). The garden was thus in the back part of the lot, and grew not only vegetables, but also fruit trees and some vines, as in the House of the Surgeon or the House of Sallust. Even smaller houses had at least a corner for herbs and flowers, which shows the general desire for green space. The peristyle garden had its origins in the peristyles (arcades) of Greek houses, which the Romans adopted in the late second century BC, and greened by means of artificial irrigation (House of Sallust, House of the Vettii, House of Polybius). These gardens were now no longer only kitchen gardens, but also decorative and pleasure gardens, for which the plural word *horti* was common, even if the Romans did not make the distinction until the height of the imperial era. If one or several porticos (columned halls or arcades) enclosed the garden, it was called a *xystus*, which often extended as a terrace in front of the

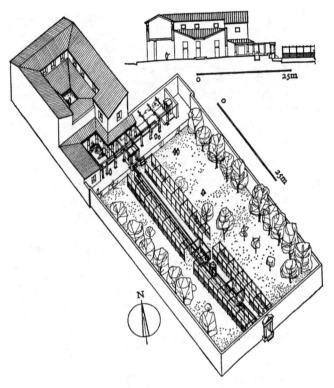

Fig. 14 House and garden of Loreius Tiburtinus in Pompeii.

longitudinal facade of a country house.[1] The walled garden was called a *viridarium* (pleasure garden or park).

The Romans generally built deep, long gardens edged in by three walls. In the centre or on the main axis, there was often a fountain, basin, channel or pathway. The so-called House of Loreius Tiburtinus (in fact D. Octavius Quartio) in Pompeii has a central axis with nested frame motifs in the form of pavilion elements and pergolas, and a euripus – a lengthy irrigation channel (Figs. 14 and 15) – so that the view from the private chambers into the garden was directed by architectural aesthetics. In addition, the garden was furnished with sculptures, vases, garden furniture and fences of wickerwork between the beds. Often the landscape was continued as a painting at the rear of the garden, or inside the house, with garden and animal paintings. In the garden itself a *triclinium* might

[1] Gieré 1986, 107ff., 284ff.

Fig. 15 House and garden of Loreius Tiburtinus in Pompeii.

also be built under arbours (Casa del Bracciale d'Oro). Thus did the garden also serve as a venue for cultured conversation and social representation.

The Romans developed a rich and significant art of garden landscaping. The profession of garden landscaper (*topiarius*) is attested from the first century BC (Cic. *ad Q. fr.* 3.1.5: 54 BC; Plin. *nat.* 12.22). According to Pliny the Elder (*nat.* 12.13), the Roman C. Matius invented the art of clipping shrubbery during Augustus' reign. Moreover, gardens provided ever new inspiration for painters and poets. If Martial (first century AD) dreamed of the garden in the city (*epigr.* 12.57: *rus in urbe*), he thus projected nature into the city in verse form.

Horticulture was an important branch of agriculture in antiquity, and an element of self-sufficiency. The garden was described as 'the peasant's second side of bacon' (Cic. *Cato* 16.56). It provided an important contribution to the diet, and thus supplemented the cultivation of fields growing the staple food, cereals. Wine and olive oil, which were basic foodstuffs too, were also produced here, particularly in city gardens. Cato (*agr.* 9) in the second century BC mentions suburban gardens with fruit trees, grapes and olives; apples and pears were later joined by cherries, which were imported from the Black Sea in 74 BC (Plin. *nat.* 15.102), along with apricots from Armenia and peaches from Persia. Figs, too, were of great importance (Cat. *agr.* 10), and were cultivated in many varieties. Thus a great variety of exotic plants found their way into the gardens, along with the native plants.

Pliny the Elder starts his work on botany (*Natural History*, books 12–17) with a discussion of trees, distinguishing 'exotic trees' (12–13), 'fruit trees' (14–15), 'forest trees' (16) and 'cultivated trees' (17); book 18 then covers agriculture; book 19, garden plants; and books 20 to 27, medical remedies from plants. In book 19.51 the garden is described as the 'farm of the poor man', from which the people obtained its sustenance. Columella too, in books 10 and 11.3 of his treatise on agriculture, *De Rustica*, discusses horticulture in some detail. Pliny saw such vegetables as cabbage, lettuce, onions, cress, leeks, cucumbers, carrots and radishes, which could be eaten raw or preserved, as important for the food supply (*nat.* 19.57ff.). Other garden plants mentioned in the sources, and whose remains have been found in Pompeii, include many evergreens: ivy, boxwood, laurel, myrtle, cypress, acanthus, dwarf plantains, rosemary and oleander, as well as flowers – lilies, roses, chrysanthemums and violets – which brought some colour into the garden, but generally had a rather subordinate role; they are also shown on the fresco with the garden scene in the Casa del Bracciale d'Oro. The use of the plants is multifaceted, as Pliny points out. Plant finds have revealed culinary, medical and ornamental species: laurel and ivy served for wreaths, and oleander both for ornamentation and against snakebites.

Archaeobotanical finds (root holes, pollen, seeds etc.) attest to a mixture of trees, vines and vegetables for the gardens of Pompeii, where trees and vines could serve as shading. The House of Polybius had fig trees, fruit trees, an olive tree with a ladder, and rows of trees and hazelnut

bushes along the garden wall. The house with the ship *Europa* had a
commercially used fruit and vegetable garden with beds and pathways; 416
root holes and 28 clay jugs along the wall have been certified, together
with vines, field beans, hazelnuts and figs. In the garden of the *caupona*
(inn) of Euxinus, near the amphitheatre, there were 2 trees, 32 vines and a
roofed *triclinium*, where the wine of the house was apparently also
served.[2]

In Rome itself there were some seventy city and villa parks, in addition
to the house gardens.[3] Luxury villas (*domus*) contained the largest green
spaces in the city, even if they were located mainly at the outskirts or in
the surrounding hills (see Fig. 22 below). The preference for luxurious
estates in Rome apparently began in the first century BC with Lucullus and
Pompey, the victors over the Hellenistic rulers of the east, and was
continued by many such personalities as Sallust, Caesar, Maecenas and
so on. Since the Roman gardens and parks were in private hands, they
were accessible to the public only to a limited extent, for example, when
rich patrons opened them up for their clients, or sponsored the establish-
ment of such a park for the public (Porticus Pompeiana: Mart. *epigr.*
2.14.10). Caesar and Agrippa, Augustus' son-in-law, friend and army
commander, bequeathed their gardens to the people in their wills (Suet.
Iul. 83; Dio 44.35.3, 54.29.4). Occasionally, Roman emperors and emp-
resses took over private gardens and put up buildings in them for public
entertainment, such as thermal springs or the so-called Naumachia on the
right bank of the Tiber, a water basin designed for the performance of
naval battles (Suet. *Aug.* 43). The imperial palaces and villas also had
splendid gardens, both in Rome itself (the Domus Augustana with its
hippodrome on the Palatine) and in Tivoli (the Villa Hadriana, early
second century AD).

All in all, the gardens thus constituted an important contribution to the
Roman food supply, and to recreation in the midst of the urban hustle
and bustle. The parks and gardens brought a piece of nature into the city;
city houses were equipped with gardens as a substitute for nature. Nero's
Domus Aurea was the pinnacle in this respect: in the middle of Rome, it
was patterned after a country or lakeside villa with a garden and a water
facility, but it also drew criticism (Tac. *ann.* 15.42). And as we will see,
these rural villas of the upper class, which obstructed lake shores and
riverbanks in Italy with their gardens and parks, also became the target of
a critique of opulence.

---

[2] Jashemski 1979, 172ff., 233ff.; 1998.   [3] Grimal 1969, 107ff.; Frass 2006, 428ff.

CHAPTER 16

Animals

For the Romans, too, keeping animals was of basic economic and social importance. Under their rule, stockbreeding was intensified and expanded throughout the empire, so that new domestic animals were also introduced north of the Alps, including donkeys, mules, peacocks, pheasants and cats. Moreover, stronger draught cattle and larger horses were bred, and poultry keeping was intensified. At the same time, however, as has been shown especially for pigs, sheep, goats, cattle and geese, suitable local breeds were retained in the conquered areas.[1]

The Romans exploited animals not only for their economic but particularly also for their entertainment value. Animal parks and game enclosures (*theriotropheia*) had already been known under such Hellenistic rulers as Ptolemy II of Egypt (285–246 BC) in Alexandria (Strab. 3.36.3–4; Athen. 5.201b–c). Since the second century BC, animal enclosures (*leporaria, vivaria*), aviaries and fish ponds (*piscinae*) were also maintained on the estates of the Roman upper class. Deer and wild boar, goats and sheep were used both for purposes of show and representation, and for the hunt and food.

At the same time, the phenomenon of public animal spectacles and animal hunting spread in Rome and its empire. The Romans not only displayed animals in cages, enclosures and triumphal processions, they also staged mock animal hunts (*venationes, munera*) as an amusement in circus games and gladiator contests. Since the early second century BC, such show hunts were held for wild and exotic animals, the range of which was continually being enlarged: lions, tigers, panthers, leopards, giraffes, elephants, rhinoceros, hippopotamuses, crocodiles, snakes, bears and so on. Bloodthirsty animal fights cost the lives of vast numbers of exotic animals and threatened certain species with extinction in some areas – elephants in Libya, lions in Thessaly and hippopotamuses in the Nile swamps, according

[1] Peters 1998.

to Themistius (*or.* 10.140a; cf. Amm. Marc. 22.15.24). However, regrets about this were limited, for the *venationes* were seen as an institution vital to the state, and hence as generally positive. Strabo (2.5.33), too, had moreover noted that the hunting and capture of wild animals along the coasts of North Africa was favourable for agriculture.

The commander M. Fulvius Nobilior, in his victory celebrations over the Aetolians in 186 BC, was the first to hold a wrestling competition as well as an expensive mock animal hunt, using lions and panthers (Liv. 39.22.1–2). In 169 BC the aediles, as the proper officials, then also held games in which 63 panthers, 40 bears and some elephants were sent into the stadium (Liv. 44.18.8). The praetor Sulla presented 100 lions (Sen. *brev. vit.* 13.6; Plin. *nat.* 8.53), while the aedile M. Aemilius Scaurus in 58 BC provided 150 leopards and for the first time an Egyptian hippopotamus and 5 crocodiles for a battle to the death (Plin. *nat.* 8.64, 96). Three years later Pompey built a theatre for the inauguration of which 18 elephants, 500 lions, 410 leopards, a rhinoceros and apparently also monkeys were set against each other. Some animals, particularly elephants, might even win the sympathy of the audience, but were then killed anyway, despite a brief pardon (Cic. *ad fam.* 7.1.3; Plin. *nat.* 8.53, 64, 70f.; Dio 39.38.1–4).

At his triumphs in 46 BC, Caesar presented 400 lions, 40 elephants, several Thessalian bulls and a giraffe (Suet. *Iul.* 37; Plin. *nat.* 8.53, 182; Dio 43.22–3.) in the celebration of his victories in Africa and Egypt. In the report of his deeds (*Res gestae* 22), published posthumously as an inscription in stone, Augustus boasted of having held 26 mock animal hunts, in which 3,500 animals were killed; his successors seem to have done their best to emulate him in this. Emperor Domitian (AD 81–96) made a habit of shooting wild animals with bow and arrow at his country home in the Alban Hills:

There are many who have more than once seen him slay a hundred wild beasts of different kinds on his Alban estate, and purposely kill some of them with two successive shots in such a way that the arrows gave the effect of horns. Sometimes he would have a slave stand at a distance and hold out the palm of his right hand for a mark, with the fingers spread; then he directed his arrows with such accuracy that they passed harmlessly between the fingers. (Suet. *Dom.* 19; Loeb)

Emperor Gordian III (AD 238–44) maintained a game enclosure at the Porta Praenestina (Hist. Aug. *Gord.* 33.1) in Rome, today's Porta Maggiore, with 32 elephants, 10 elks, 10 tigers, 60 lions, 30 leopards, 10 hyenas, 6 hippopotamuses, a rhinoceros, 10 white or wild lions, 10 giraffes, 20 wild asses and 20 wild horses, all of whom fell victim to the 'Millennium Games' in AD 248, held to celebrate the thousandth anniversary of the founding of Rome. The first bans on arena fights were imposed during the fourth century AD, but the animal shows continued, even under Christian rule, to the end of antiquity.

Where animals were artistically represented, it was generally in a subservient role, supporting human sublimeness and power, especially at the hunt. Emperor Hadrian (AD 117–38) is shown on a tondo on the Arch of Constantine in Rome hunting boar. Sarcophagi with hunting scenes glorify the victory or *virtus* (bravery) of the noble deceased – by contrast to the dying page – and raise hope for eternal life.[2] The great hunt on the floor mosaic in the late Roman palace villa at Piazza Armerina (Sicily, *c.* AD 300) extends over 64 m of a corridor. It shows an exotic hilly landscape, with personifications of Asia and Africa in the apses: big cats kill antelopes, and wild animals are captured with nets and ropes and, under the supervision of imperial officials, loaded onto ships for transport to Italy in rolling cages.[3]

It can generally be noted that there was a paradoxical relationship between human and animal, characterised on the one hand by personal attachment and care, and on the other by baiting and exploitation. The animal kingdom was seen as exemplary, even in Vergil's parable of the well-organised bee colony (*georg.* 4.149–227, esp. 220). Pliny the Elder dedicated four books of his 37-volume *Natural History* to zoology, and at the beginning (8.1) described the elephant as most similar to humans. Even if the animals were part of nature, humans still remained the main point of reference. They could still dispose of animals, although the philosophers might admonish them to deal gently with them.[4]

The Neopythagoreans opposed anthropocentrism and stood for the protection of animals and for vegetarianism. For Plutarch, animals by nature had greater capacity for virtue and moderation than humans (*mor.* 987b–f, 988f–991d); moreover, they had natural intelligence and reason (991f–992a). Eating meat was described as harmful (995c–996a), so as to prevent senseless butchering for pleasure's sake (997d–e). Finally, Porphyrius (*c.* AD 234–305/10) too expressly rejected the eating of meat (*abst.* 3.1ff.). Early Christianity and the New Testament brought about a certain association of animals with the divine inasmuch as animal sacrifice was abolished, and animals had positive connotations at least symbolically as a part of creation: the Lamb of God, the Holy Ghost as a dove and the Good Shepherd.

---

[2] Toynbee 1973, 65–6, 132; Andreae 1985; W. Martini, 'Römische Antike', in Dinzelbacher 2000, 91ff.
[3] Gentili 1999, III.   [4] Sorabji 1993, 178–9, 183–4, 208–9; Gilhus 2006, 44ff., 64ff.

CHAPTER 17

Food

The Romans had terms for breakfast, lunch and supper – *ientaculum*, *prandium* and *cena* – the first two of which were seen as only minor meals and were mainly eaten cold. In the morning, water with bread and cheese, and sometimes also eggs, olives, capers or milk and honey, would be taken. The midday meal too might be limited to a piece of bread with cheese or cold or smoked meat, vegetables and fruit, with water or wine as the main drink. The main meal was the evening *cena*, which was often celebrated in grand style by the upper classes, and to which its members invited one another. The wealthy had a room in their houses especially for this purpose, the *triclinium*, where men and women dined in recline, while the children sat. The order of the three slightly rising couch beds, each for three persons, was graded hierarchically; attendants served the meal.[1]

A complete *cena* included three parts. The appetiser (*gustatio*) was usually served cold, and consisted of salads, raw vegetables, eggs and fish or seafood. The main course included dishes of cooked vegetables and meat. The dessert (*secunda mensa*) contained pastries and fruits. The process of the evening meal was ritualised, with an initial offering of wine opening the feast. After the *gustatio* came a drink of honey wine (*mulsum*); following each course, the drinking bowls were filled with various other wines. After the main course, an offering was made to the *lares*, the tutelary gods of the house. Following the *cena*, a banquet would continue with a *comissatio*, a round of drinking with fixed customs, in which the drinking bowl was passed round for a variety of toasts. Such a banquet (*convivium*) could therefore last eight to ten hours, or until dawn, accompanied by many presentations, such as music, dance and games.[2]

The productive provinces exported more than cereals, wine and oil to Rome; other foods, including delicacies, were transported over long

---

[1] Holliger 1996, 5–6, 55ff.; Fellmeth 2001, 87ff.   [2] Carcopino 1992, 360ff. (304ff. in 1939 edn).

distances throughout the empire, so that various products came from specialised areas: particularly fish sauce (*garum*) from Spain, sausages from Gaul, spices from the East, lemons and pomegranates from Africa, dates from the oases, plums from Damascus and oysters from the North Sea. Wine, fish sauce and oil were transported in amphorae, which were then disposed of on a gigantic, ever growing – and stinking – mountain of shards on the bank of the Tiber south of Rome – today's Monte Testaccio. These food transports could thus certainly have damaging environmental effects, at least locally. All in all, this trade contributed to the spread of Mediterranean cuisine, even if regional traditions and preferences survived in the provinces.[3]

Water and wine were the chief beverages, although in some provinces, including Egypt, Spain and Gaul (Plin. *nat.* 22.164), beer, which was cheaper, and disdained in Rome, was preferred. It was seen as the drink of the poor, while wine from Italy was initially consumed only by the rich (Athen. 152c). In Egypt, beer was accepted, but was supplemented by wine, which was also increasingly exported to Rome.[4]

There were many different kinds of wine, from the first-class Falernian to the inferior Vatican and Marseillian; these were in some cases sweetened by thickened grape and fruit juice which had been boiled in lead vessels (Plin. *nat.* 14.68, 80, 130; Mart. *epigr.* 9.93, 10.36, 45). In that way, lead could enter the wine and have damaging health effects. Resin or pitch might also be added as preservatives, and the amphorae sealed. For drinking, the wine was sifted into a mixing jug, diluted with cold or warmed water, and finally poured into bowls. The problems caused by cutting wine were known (Plin. *nat.* 14.68, 130) but were never systematically addressed – as we will see below, too, in the case of lead in the water pipes.

The food of the common Romans was for the most part vegetarian. In Italy, emmer (*triticum dicoccoides*) was seen as one of the oldest foods (Plin. *nat.* 18.62, 83), but was increasingly being replaced by bread wheat (*triticum aestivum*).[5] The typical food of the poor was dark, ground barley bread, or a mash (*puls*) of water, oil and barley; wheat, used for baking light bread, was better and more expensive. In addition, fruit and vegetables (cabbage, garlic, onions, beets), legumes (beans, lentils and pea mash, sometimes enriched with pork bacon), cheese (*moretum*: herb cheese), eggs and marinated fish were also consumed; meat was rare, since it was generally too expensive. Such simple food was, however, also seen

---

[3] Thüry 2004, 29.   [4] André 1981, 177–8; Garnsey 1999, 118–19.
[5] André 1981, 51–2; Garnsey 1999, 120.

as proof of cultivation and moderation; Seneca too supported it (*epist.* 2.17–18). Even Emperor Trajan (AD 98–117) held modest *cenae,* accompanied by refined performances and conversations (Plin. *paneg.* 49.5ff.).

Recipes were in circulation even in early imperial times. Around AD 400, they were compiled under the name Apicius into a diverse collection, *De re coquinaria,* which, unlike modern recipes, often contains only very rudimentary indications as to quantities. A basic difference from the modern diet is the lack of sugar and the low use of salt, which was largely obtained from the sea and used mainly as a preservative. Honey and fish sauce (*garum*) took their place. There were of course no potatoes, tomatoes or maize, and very little rice.

The calculation of portions and calories in the Roman diet depends particularly on information from the first half of the second century BC from Cato (*agr.* 56ff.), who gives us considerable figures: while an estate administrator was allocated 0.7 kg of wheat and 0.57 litres of wine per day, a working slave might be issued 1.6 kg of wheat bread and 0.72 litres of wine, which, together with the oil, would come to approximately 2,700 and 4,900 kcal, respectively. According to the historian Polybius (6.39), a soldier in the mid-second century BC would get approximately 35 litres or 27 kg of wheat a month, or 0.9 kg per day, which would mean approximately 2,990 kcal. Moreover, soldiers frequently received bacon, cheese, salt, vinegar and hardtack (Hist. Aug. *Avid.* 5.3). Late Roman papyri from Egypt give the daily ration of a soldier as three Roman pounds (969 g) of bread, two pounds (646 g) of meat or bacon, 1.1 litres of wine and 0.7 decilitres of oil.[6]

The situation in the capital, Rome, where Gaius Gracchus in 123/2 BC introduced food distribution and also built corn storage houses for this purpose, was quite different (Plut. *C. Gracch.* 6–7). In the first century BC the poorer citizens, the corn recipients, were issued approximately 44 litres of wheat a month, that is, little more than the workers and slaves as recommended by Cato (approximately 35–9 litres). W. M. Jongman calculates rations of 33 kg, based on a total quantity meant to supply 360,000 people; he also assumes somewhat optimistically that half of the caloric requirement of the Romans had already been covered just by the olive oil and wine.[7] However, it is also necessary to take into account that the corn recipients had to feed their families with the allocated rations, and initially also had to pay a certain sum for them, amounting to several days'

[6] Garnsey and Saller 1987, 89–90; Junkelmann 1997, 87.   [7] Jongman 2007, 602ff.

Fig. 16 Tavern in the Thermopolium of the via di Diana in Ostia.

earnings.[8] Sallust accordingly called the allocation 'prison rations' (*hist.* 3.48.19). Moreover, Caesar and Augustus restricted the number of recipients to 150,000 and 200,000, respectively (Suet. *Iul.* 41; Dio 55.10.1), so that a major portion of the city, which now had over a million inhabitants, was cut off from the distribution; scarcity and malnutrition occasionally occurred.[9]

It is commonly held that the lower classes of urban society ate in taverns, which was not universally the case. Taverns generally had an L-shaped bar facing the street, which could be equipped with up to six *dolia* (large earthenware vessels) as food containers (Figs. 16 and 17). Remains of the ancient contents indicate pea soup in Pompeii, and vegetables and cereals in Herculaneum. Stoves could be built into the bar, or separately. On the sides were masonry steps or wall shelves on which drinking cups, glasses, dishes and vessels were kept. Such tavern units were sometimes combined with other rooms, and could then serve as inns (*popinae, hospitia, stabula*), or else they were only a part of a private house.[10]

---

[8] von Ungern-Sternberg 1991.   [9] Garnsey 1988, 218ff.; Robinson 1992, 151ff.
[10] Kleberg 1966.

Fig. 17 Thermopolium of the via di Diana in Ostia.

A *popina* is assumed to have encompassed at least three rooms: a kitchen, a dining room and a tavern unit. A *hospitium* additionally offered overnight accommodation, sometimes with a *stabulum* for wagons and horses in the backyard. Such taverns and inns have rarely been archaeologically substantiated in the provinces but are nevertheless attested, for example by gravestones with pub scenes in Augsburg and Regensburg. Written sources also indicate that hostels (*mansiones*) were available for travellers in the countryside, and were also used by the upper classes (Hor. *sat.* 1.5; Mart. *epigr.* 6.94).

Overall, there was a broad range of restaurant facilities, which were in some cases also used by the wealthy; however, they could never replace the private banquet at home. On the other hand, it is questionable how many of the plebeians or members of the lower classes could afford a meal in a tavern; after all, at least those citizens in the capital who were entitled to a state allotment of cereals could process it themselves or have it baked into bread. In the countryside, the situation was different, inasmuch as the rural population was self-sufficient.

CHAPTER 18

Fire and water

FIRES IN ROME

Fire had religious significance in Rome, and was used in ritualistic veneration. The Volcanalia festivities were held every August in honour of the god of fire, Volcanus. In Rome the qualities of Hestia, the Greek goddess of the hearth, were embodied in the Latin goddess Vesta, goddess of the state hearth. A round temple at the forum Romanum was consecrated to her, as the central place of the community. Here there was a hearth with the eternal fire, tended by the Vestal Virgins, who were in priestly service. The shrine was at the same time the state's storage house, and was under the protection of the Penates, whose religious image (*palladium*) was kept here. The six Vestal Virgins enjoyed great honours and privileges, since they embodied purity and thus enabled expiation. Since their virgin inviolability symbolised stored fertility, they were important for growth and fertility rites. Their supreme duty besides their virginity was the guardianship of the eternal fire, as an expression of community. If the fire was extinguished, they risked being flogged (Dion. Hal. 2.67).

For Rome there was also a rational, political aspect of fire, since it could be used as an instrument of power. As in the case of water, the sources primarily refer to the capital itself. In the course of the growth of the city, the danger of fire was addressed organisationally. This at the same time lent political authority to those involved in such activities, since fires had been frequent during the Roman republic. Numerous major conflagrations are reported, particularly toward the end of the republic: in 50 BC an enormous blaze destroyed numerous districts (fourteen *vici*), and the next year there was an earthquake accompanied by fires which destroyed many residential areas.[1] It was the time that the old republican system was

---

[1] Kolb 1995, 286.

breaking apart; senatorial rule had proven incapable of addressing the problems facing Rome and its empire, and the ruling elite was engaged in constant internal strife. In this situation Caesar seized power with his army and began to reorganise the state, but was then murdered in 44 BC.

The danger of fire in the city of Rome was due mainly to the fact that wood was still the most widespread building material for simple housing. Problems were caused not only by hearths, but also by numerous open flames, such as candles, torches, oil lamps, and coal basins for heating and cooking. These threatened wooden ceilings and wooden partitions in the upper storeys, which were installed by profit-hungry landlords to create additional rental space, for in the narrow streets and high buildings the housing shortage was acute. The politician and financier M. Licinius Crassus (115–53 BC) had a gang of 500 construction workers and was also involved in real estate speculation. He would buy houses which were already on fire, or were located near a potential source of fire, and then build new, profitable tenement blocks on the vacant lots (Plut. *Crass.* 2.34).

During the republican period, there were no effective regulations for home building, nor did insurance or any firefighting or police forces exist. Fire prevention was inadequately handled by a fire watch of only a few people, the *tresviri nocturni,* who were responsible for public order at night, and a small gang of state slaves, who were completely ineffective in cases of major fires. For this reason neighbourly assistance was widespread, and private efforts required. M. Egnatius Rufus, who held the office of aedile in 22 or 21 BC, with responsibility for the supervision of streets, squares and markets, had in previous years assigned both his own and rented slaves to firefighting, and thus achieved great popularity. However, Augustus, who had taken power in 27 BC as the new ruler, accused him of conspiracy and had him killed (Vell. 2.91.3).

Augustus, Rome's first emperor, only gradually took measures against the danger of fires. First, in 23 BC, he set up a fire brigade, for which a few *vigiles* ('guardians') were drafted and subordinated to the aediles. This organisation was initially very rudimentary, and hence inefficient. In 7 BC, Rome was reorganised, with the city's four traditional regions being replaced by fourteen regions and some 265 *vici*; at this time, the firefighting force too was restructured. The small neighbourhoods were given a local autonomous administration under *collegia* consisting of four *vicomagistri* each, recruited from the lower classes of society, or from freedmen.[2]

After more major conflagrations, Augustus in AD 6 organised seven cohorts as a permanent fire brigade, with each cohort responsible for two of the fourteen urban regions. These paramilitary units, with a total of 7,000 freedmen, were directly under the command of a *praefectus vigilum* from the equestrian class, who was appointed by the emperor and directly responsible to him (Dio 52.24.6, 33.1, 55.26.4–5). This professional unit not only strengthened the city's firefighting capabilities: it also provided a permanent presence of law and order for the ruler at the neighbourhood level. There were seven barracks as guard houses at the city wall, and smaller guard-stations distributed throughout the city. These troops nevertheless had a largely preventive function, since they were powerless against a heavy fire. Here, Augustus' construction regulations, which limited the height of houses to 70 feet (20.7 m), or about six or seven storeys, were little help, either (Strab. 5.3.7).

The best known fire in Rome broke out on the night of 18/19 July AD 64, and lasted for nine days. Emperor Nero (AD 54–68), who had been staying in Antium, hurried to Rome and initiated relief activities. The rumour nevertheless arose that he had ordered the fire set himself (Tac. *ann.* 15.38–44). Thereafter, blame for the disaster was laid upon the Christians, who were hated by the majority of the people, and who suffered severe punishments as a result. Only four of the fourteen regions had escaped the fire; three had been completely burned to the ground, while in seven more only a few houses remained. The building rubble was disposed of in the marshes of Ostia. The number of human victims is unknown; it must be assumed that several thousand died.

After the fire catastrophe of AD 64, the most comprehensive attempt was made to rebuild and modernise Rome's residential neighbourhoods (Tac. *ann.* 15.43). In place of the narrow, twisted lanes, Nero had more regular, broader streets built, with arcades in front of the houses. To prevent new fires, common walls of adjacent buildings and combustible materials were to be avoided; fire-proof building blocks were used, and fire-extinguishing equipment provided. Under Trajan, the height of buildings was still further limited, to only 60 feet (17.7 m) (Aur. Vict. *epit. Caes.* 13.13). These measures were, however, of only limited success,

---

[2] Robinson 1992, 105–6.

for the streets remained narrow and twisted. The fire hazard could never really be eliminated, so that fires occurred repeatedly.

THE WATER SUPPLY AND SEWAGE SYSTEM OF ROME

The logistical problems of the city included water supply and sewage disposal. Rome's water supply was relatively good at an early date, even including a certain level of hygiene. Here the Romans used achievements which we have already observed among the Greeks. Originally, drinking water had been obtained from the Tiber and from wells; from the late fourth century BC it was supplied by means of ever longer and higher aqueducts.

During the republic four such aqueducts were built: the aqua Appia (312 BC), the Anio Vetus (272 BC), the aqua Marcia (144–140 BC) and the aqua Tepula (126 BC), which brought in water from the Anio Valley, or, in the case of the aqua Tepula, from the Alban Hills (Fig. 18). The water arrived in the city by way of the surrounding hills, where it was stored in reservoirs known as *castellae*, and then distributed via clay and lead pipes to the lower-lying residential areas. Despite this flow-through system, the water was not wasted, but was intercepted repeatedly or fed into households and gardens. Initially, of course, very little overflow water was passed on to private households, for the goal was not the comprehensive supply of all houses, but rather the supply of public wells with drinking water.[3]

As early as the sixth century BC, the Roman Forum had been drained and the Cloaca Maxima built, a large central sewer which emptied into the Tiber. It was the most important sewer during the next centuries, and was continually expanded – in some parts, it is used to this day. By the first century BC an extensive system of sewage ditches existed, which, however, also brought with it a number of dangers. Problems included their stench in dry spells, the backup of the sewer system when the water of the Tiber was high (Plin. *nat.* 36.105) and the inadequate clearage of the sewage ditches of waste material. The ditches not only provided a cleaning function, but were also sources of gases of decomposition and pathogens which repeatedly caused epidemics.[4] The only way to counteract this was with a massive flushing, which apparently also contributed to the improvement of air quality (Front. *aqu.* 88, 111).

---

[3] G. Garbrecht, 'Wasserversorgungstechnik in römischer Zeit', in Frontinus-Gesellschaft 1989, 32ff.
[4] Robinson 1992, 112–13.

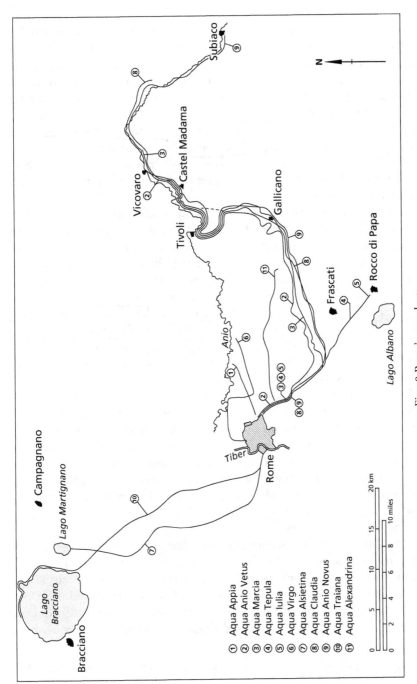

Fig. 18 Rome's aqueducts.

① Aqua Appia
② Aqua Anio Vetus
③ Aqua Marcia
④ Aqua Tepula
⑤ Aqua Iulia
⑥ Aqua Virgo
⑦ Aqua Alsietina
⑧ Aqua Claudia
⑨ Aqua Anio Novus
⑩ Aqua Traiana
⑪ Aqua Alexandrina

Bracciano

Lago
Bracciano

Campagnano

Lago Martignano

Tiber

Rome

Anio

Tivoli

Vicovaro

Castel Madama

Gallicano

Subiaco

Frascati

Rocco di Papa

Lago Albano

N

0   5   10   15   20 km
0   2   4   6   8   10 miles

In 312 BC the state assumed overall responsibility for the water supply, which was thus no longer a family problem, but a communal task. This was financed by war spoils, and managed by regular officials: the censors, who were chosen every five years and were responsible, among other things, for public procurement; the aediles; and in some cases special commissions. Unlike many other cities, Rome was no longer exclusively dependent on the generosity of individuals. The state built aqueducts and made water available to the public free of charge. Connections of private homes to the water system were seen as privileges for persons who had distinguished themselves, and apparently had to be approved by the people's assembly.[5]

By 126 BC, however, after the first four aqueducts were built, construction largely came to a standstill. No definite authority yet existed for the maintenance of the aqueducts; the traditional offices, the aediles and censors, were soon overwhelmed by the task. By the end of the republic, therefore, there was need for action, and Augustus, the first emperor, reacted accordingly. A new principle was now imposed: private persons paid for the maintenance of the water system, that is, it was paid for by private donations from the emperor or other members of the ruling class.

M. Vipsanius Agrippa, a friend of Augustus since their youth, who had led the victory over Anthony and Cleopatra at Actium in 31 BC and became Augustus' son-in-law ten years later, took over responsibility for the water supply. He used his own funds to expand and maintain the water lines, a kind of propagandistic donation to the Roman plebeians. He may already have begun to do so when he served as praetor in 40 BC, but this was definitely the case when he assumed the position of aedile in 33 BC (Front. *aqu.* 9) – specifically for that purpose. New aqueducts, the aqua Iulia (33 BC, possibly started in 40 BC) and the aqua Virgo (21–19 BC) were built; the latter provided the water for the first public thermal baths on the Campus Martius. This considerably increased the amount of water being supplied to Rome.

Agrippa acted with senate approval, but at his own authority and expense. He assigned 240 of his own slaves to duty as so-called *aquaria*, and thus laid the foundations for a professional administration of the water supply; he also became the number two man in the state. At the same time, he probably introduced the system of standardised lead pipes (*quinariae*), which was used during the imperial era, and was a

[5] W. Eck, 'Organisation und Administration der Wasserversorgung Roms', in Frontinus-Gesellschaft 1989, 63–4.

prerequisite for the comprehensive provision of water system connections for private residences (Front. *aqu.* 25ff.).[6]

After Agrippa's death in 12 BC, Augustus felt forced to take responsibility for the water supply personally. His goal was to underpin Agrippa's privately financed efforts by state action. Agrippa's slaves were therefore transferred to the state, and received the designation *familia publica* as public servants. Agrippa's regulations were published as an edict. Moreover, various senate resolutions passed in 11 BC, as well as the *lex Quinctia* of 9 BC, created a solid legal basis for the administration of the aqueducts (Front. *aqu.* 125ff.). The *lex Quinctia* stipulated the protection of the aqueducts and banned the theft of water. A *cura aquarum* was also established in 11 BC: the emperor appointed three distinguished men of the senatorial class (consulars, i.e., former consuls) for unlimited terms as *curatores aquarum* to run the water supply, and provided them with public employees. Their tasks included the preservation of the structures and staff supervision, approval procedure for private connections to the system, and the legal handling of disputes and offences (Front. *aqu.* 98ff.).

During the later part of Augustus' reign, the aqua Alsietina and several other canals named 'Augusta' were built (Front. *aqu.* 11–12). The lines were in some places marked with stones (*cippi*) every 70 m, for better monitoring. The Alsietina, on the right bank of the Tiber, in the area of today's Trastevere, fed the Naumachia, the gigantic water basin for the performance of mock naval battles and similar entertainments (Front. *aqu.* 11). Overall, the quantity of water introduced into the capital more than doubled under Augustus. The first Roman emperor had successfully accomplished the smooth transfer of this public task to his personal responsibility, without offending the senate; a state function thus fell under the aegis of the emperor. Accordingly, private connections to the water system were no longer allocated by the people's assembly but by the emperor himself. Access to water was now granted by special permission from the emperor, as a *beneficium*, so that it was no longer merit, but rather imperial favour, that determined private advantage.[7]

The constantly recurring floods of the Tiber, which could inundate entire neighbourhoods of Rome and cause substantial damage, were also a problem. Caesar was said to have already made plans to dam and rechannel the Tiber extensively (Cic. *Att.* 13.33.1; Plut. *Caes.* 58.4). The Tiber bed had been cleaned under Augustus to achieve better drainage of the water

[6] Evans 1982.
[7] Eck, 'Organisation und Administration', in Frontinus-Gesellschaft 1989, 66–7.

masses and of the overflow channels (Suet. *Aug.* 30). In AD 15, after a severe flood, the emperor Tiberius, Augustus' successor, appointed five curators to supervise the bed and banks of the Tiber (*curatores alvei et riparum Tiberis*), and two senators to draft a comprehensive regulation plan (Dio 57.14.7–8). This included the damming of tributaries: the Chiana (then known as the Clanis) was to be redirected from the Tiber into the Arno; the water of the Nera, too, was to be diverted; and the Veline Lake was to be dammed, instead of flowing into the Nera. However, the local residents feared inundations and also expressed religious concerns, so that the project was ultimately dropped (Tac. *ann.* 1.76, 79). The Tiber continued to cause great damage on its way to the sea (Plin. *epist.* 8.17).[8]

Thereafter, Emperor Claudius (AD 41–54) instituted the office of *procurator aquarum* (Front. *aqu.* 105) in Rome as a kind of executive alongside the commissioners of the *cura aquarum*. The staff was enlarged with 460 imperial slaves and freedmen (*familia Caesaris*: Front. *aqu.* 116), so that the water authority had the largest number of public employees (700). The number of aqueducts was again increased by two, the aqua Claudia and the Anio Novus (AD 38–52).

Emperor Nerva in AD 97 appointed Sextus Julius Frontinus as *curator aquarum*. He wrote the work *De aquaeductu urbis Romae*, which describes the aqueducts, the distribution of water and the applicable legal rules. The water quality of the various mains is also assessed (*aqu.* 89ff.), and the punishment for pollution mentioned (*aqu.* 97). Based on his account (*aqu.* 78), the daily capacity for the first century AD has been estimated at approximately 500,000–600,000 cu. m;[9] together with the two last lines built, the aqua Traiana (AD 109–17) and the aqua Alexandrina (AD 226), it might even have reached 1 million cu. m, or approximately 500–600 or even 1,000 litres per head per day – approximately double or even four times today's capacity. However, this calculation took into account only the flow area, not the flow velocity. A more recent estimate by C. Bruun arrives at only 67 litres per day,[10] so that no safe assessment can be made here.

Under Frontinus the aqueduct system had a total length of 423 km and included 247 reservoirs and 591 open water pools. One-sixth of the water went to the emperor, a third to homes and the rest to the public (Front. *aqu.* 78). The emperor not only decided upon the allocation to private persons, but also levied the charges; standardised lead pipes of various

---

[8] Aldrete 2007, 15.   [9] Garbrecht 1984, 8.   [10] Bruun 1991, 103.

Fig. 19 Herodian Roman aqueduct in Caesarea, Israel.

sizes connected homes to the distributor, and their dimensions served as a basis for calculating the water rates. The pipes (*fistulae*) were labelled by name and mainly belonged to senators, and also to equestrians and imperial freedmen.[11] Disposal of sewage was provided by the underground sewer system, flushed by water from the aqueducts, which, however, simply shifted the problem of pollution from Rome to the lower reaches of the Tiber.

HYDRAULIC ENGINEERING, WATER POISONING AND LEAD PROBLEMS

Outside Rome, too, important water mains were built during the Augustan period, including the aqueducts of Emerita Augusta (Mérida) and Tarragona in Spain, Pont du Gard in Gaul, the canals of Alexandria, and the water supply systems of Pompeii and of Caesarea in Judaea (Fig. 19). In addition to aqueducts and municipal distribution networks, the Romans in various areas around the Mediterranean built valley dams such as those familiar in Egypt and the Near East, one example being Emerita Augusta,[12] and systems of canals, with which entire areas could be irrigated artificially, such as in the Po Valley (Strab. 4.6.7, 5.1.4; Plin. *nat.* 3.119). Lakes and marshes were also drained, for example the Veline Lake in the third century BC (Cic. *Att.* 4.15.5), the Fucine Lake under Claudius (Suet. *Claud.* 20; Tac. *ann.* 12.56) and Hadrian (Hist. Aug. *Hadr.* 22.12),

[11] Bruun 1991, 77ff.   [12] Schnitter 1978, 1994.

the Po delta (Strab. 5.1.11; Plin. *nat.* 3.120–1), parts of Tuscany, and the Pontine marshes in Latium (Liv. *epit.* 46). Numerous canals and river regulation projects served navigation, including the Fossa Mariana in the Rhone delta, and the Fossa Drusiana between the Rhine and the Ijssel in the Netherlands, or else were built to protect settlements from flooding, as in the case of Glanum (Saint-Rémy-de-Provence, France).

It was generally recommended to provide farm fields with drainage ditches and irrigation canals (Cat. *agr.* 155.1; Verg. *georg.* 1.106–10), for which there were precise legal stipulations (Dig. 8.3.1ff., 39.3.8ff., 43.20.1ff.). The property owners adjacent to water mains and bodies of waters were required to ensure that the water, a public asset, remained accessible to all, particularly for navigation and leased fishing. Any modifications that caused the water of a public stream to take a different course than it had in the previous summer were generally banned (Dig. 43.13.1ff.). On the other hand, hardly any measures were taken against water pollution by sewage.

Not only in Rome were sewage ditches an important factor for waste disposal. In Pompeii the high kerbstones and the 'zebra crossings' made of stone blocks show that, on the one hand, rain and sewage were drained away there and that, on the other, overflow water was fed through to clean the streets. Urban streets were provided with underground sewers to wash away excrement; however, these sewers never constituted a full-coverage network, and in some cities they did not exist at all, so that much waste was left in the streets (Strab. 14.1.37). In some places it has been observed that the waste in the streets was therefore periodically covered over with new layers of gravel, as in Augusta Raurica (Augst, Switzerland) and Coblenz, Germany.[13]

A number of places in the Roman world faced problems of water pollution and water poisoning due to the practice of waste disposal by way of water. Even in Hellenistic times there had been a case of mass poisoning of the Nile, with numerous deaths (Athen. 2.42a). Fish from dirty rivers were generally considered bad (Gal. *alim. fac.* 3.24[25], 28–9[29–30]). Pliny the Elder reported on a number of poisoned rivers (*nat.* 18.3), and his nephew Pliny the Younger wanted to have the Amastris (Amasra) River in Pontus-Bithynia covered over because of the danger of epidemics (*epist.* 10.98–9). Moreover, the numerous military camps in the Roman Empire seem to have regularly contaminated the water of their surroundings (Veg. *mil.* 3.2). Apparently, no measures to prevent such problems were taken.

---

[13] Thüry 2001, 23ff.

Another threat to the people was the lead in the metal pipes, which polluted the drinking water. Such lead pipes existed as water supply mains in settlements throughout the Roman Empire; they were economically advantageous over clay pipes. While the harmful effects of lead pipes had been recognised early (Vitr. 8.6.10–11), the problem was never addressed systematically. Convenience, which particularly benefited the upper classes, the consumers of luxury goods, was not the only determining factor. It has to be taken into account, however, that the inside surface of lead pipes was often rapidly covered with a layer of calcium, so that the metal could no longer enter the drinking water. Moreover, Rome itself was supplied with hard water, which took up a very low level of contamination. Skeleton examinations from throughout the Roman Empire have yielded a wide range of different results with regard to lead poisoning, some considerably above, others far below, today's values.[14] Thus, even if the lead caused health problems locally, it had no noticeable effect on the population as a whole.[15]

[14] Drasch 1982.   [15] Weeber 1990, 171ff.

CHAPTER 19

Earthquakes and volcanoes

EARTHQUAKES

With the incorporation of the Mediterranean areas into the Roman Empire, Rome was increasingly confronted with the problem of earthquakes. These are reported for Italy during the time of the republic as well, in 217 and 91 BC, with Pliny even telling of simultaneous coastal inundations (*nat.* 2.199–200). For the imperial era we have more detailed reports about numerous further earthquakes at various places. After Emperor Augustus had already provided assistance to cities in Asia Minor for reconstruction in 25 BC (Strab. 12.8.18; Suet. *Tib.* 8), in AD 17 the 'twelve-city earthquake' in Asia Minor gave cause for Emperor Tiberius to provide state relief as well: Sardes received 10 million sesterces and five years' tax exemption, and similar provisions also applied to the other cities (Tac. *ann.* 2.47). An earthquake shook Campania in AD 62, which later made imperial aid from Vespasian necessary, and caused damage in Pompeii that is visible to this day (Sen. *nat.* 6.1.13ff.).[1] Seventeen years later came the devastating eruption of Mount Vesuvius.

Earthquakes shook the eastern Mediterranean particularly frequently: in AD 115 Antioch was struck by an earthquake from which Emperor Trajan was just able to escape, and during which several miraculous rescues were attested (Dio 68.24–5). In the middle of the second century AD the earth shook in Lycia, Caria, Kos and Rhodes, leading Emperor Antoninus Pius to provide help for the reconstruction of the cities there (Paus. 8.43.4; Hist. Aug. *Antonin.* 9). In AD 358 an earthquake in Nicomedia was accompanied by whirlwinds and lightning, so that many houses collapsed, fire broke out and many deaths were lamented, since no help from outside came (Amm. Marc. 17.7.1–8). And in AD 365 an

---

[1] J.-P. Adam, 'Observations techniques sur les suites du séisme de 62 à Pompéi', in Albore Livadie 1986, 67ff.

earthquake and tsunami struck the Mediterranean area, devastating Mothone in the Peloponnese and especially Alexandria (Amm. Marc. 26.10.15–19).

For Seneca the incident in Campania in AD 62 was cause for examining earthquake theory (Sen. *nat.* 6.1.3). He favoured Aristotle's 'pneumatic theory', but also believed that underground fire and water had an effect. His chief goal was to reduce the terror of such natural disasters. In the imperial era, attempts to predict earthquakes, or to prevent them by means of astrology and magic, became widespread (Plin. *nat.* 2.191ff.). Other measures too were intended to help avoid damage, such as special types of construction of foundations and walls, and a suitable choice of sites (Strab. 12.8.18; Plin. *nat.* 2.197–8). However, since no comprehensive prevention was possible, emperors could repeatedly portray themselves as rescuers in time of need, and give propagandistic proof of their benefi-cence. Even if special commissions were in some cases appointed, no permanent organisation for dealing with disasters ever emerged.[2]

THE ERUPTION OF VESUVIUS

The eruption of Mount Vesuvius in the region of the Gulf of Naples in AD 79 buried the Roman villa sites Oplontis, Boscoreale and Stabiae as well as the two cities of Pompeii and Herculaneum, in the midst of their flourishing everyday life, thus conserving a wealth of information for posterity (Fig. 20). Moreover, this is the first volcanic eruption in history for which a detailed eyewitness report is available – two letters from Pliny the Younger to the historian Tacitus (see below), albeit not written until some 30 years later. Together with earlier mentions of Vesuvius and later interpretations of the catastrophe, they nevertheless yield information about how people dealt with the volcano and its eruption.

The eruption of Vesuvius in AD 79 started in the late morning of 24 August. First, the volcanic plug of cooled lava was blown out; there followed the 'Plinian eruptions', named after Pliny's description: intense, continuous gas emissions which hurled large quantities of magma and lapilli – small pieces of old lava from the plug and the inner slope of the crater – up to 30 km into the air and formed a kind of pine-shaped cloud. The liquid magma was torn into small pieces by the rapid expansion and hardened in the air to porous pumice, so that a hailstorm of glowing stones fell upon Pompeii and Stabiae; during this first phase they were

---

[2] Sonnabend 1999, 220ff.

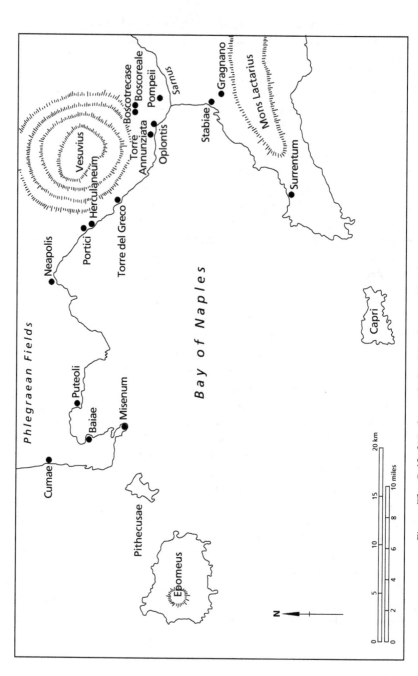

Fig. 20 The Gulf of Naples, with the cities destroyed by the eruption of Vesuvius.

buried to a depth of some 2.5 m. When the pressure eased, glowing material emerging from fissures in the mountainside ran down the slope in a pyroclastic flow. At the same time, the sputum material sparked torrential rains through condensation in the stratosphere, which in turn mixed with the lava flow to form a river of hot mud which engulfed Herculaneum and buried it to a depth of 12 to 20 m. Since the magma and the lava flows also brought forth a cloud of gas, many of the 15,000 to 20,000 residents of Pompeii who attempted to escape the disaster were then killed by suffocation, a fate which also befell Pliny the Elder. Some 2,000 inhabitants who tried to find safety in their houses and cellars died there. On 25 August came the second phase, in which a rain of ash and lapilli was dumped on the city, burying it under another layer up to 6.5 m thick.[3]

The region around the Gulf of Naples had long been densely populated, since the volcanic soil was fertile, and the area was particularly scenic. According to Strabo (5.4.8), Vesuvius was considered extinct, so that it was not feared, nor indeed perceived as a real volcano. The last eruption had occurred centuries earlier, and the earthquakes which regularly struck the region were seen as the real problem. As noted, the last great earthquake had occurred seventeen years earlier, in AD 62, and was believed to have been caused by underground winds, so that it was not seen as a harbinger of volcanic activity (Plin. *nat.* 2.192). Rebuilding was thus still well under way when Pompeii and Herculaneum disappeared apparently forever under ash and mud.

Pliny the Elder, the famous author of the *Naturalis historia*, was at that time the commander of the fleet at Misenum on the Gulf of Naples, about 30 km west of the main event (Fig. 20). On 24 August he had just welcomed his nephew, known to us as Pliny the Younger, for a visit, so that the young man was able to record his uncle's reactions in a later letter to Tacitus (*epist.* 6.16). As the eruption became visible in the Gulf of Naples, the naval commander wanted to launch a reconnaissance journey, but, in response to a call for help from an acquaintance named Rectina, sailed for Herculaneum. There, however, a muddy lava flow prevented him from landing, so that he turned towards Stabiae, where his friend Pomponianus lived, and where he died of suffocation the next morning. Pliny the Younger, who had stayed in Misenum, reported in a second letter to Tacitus (*epist.* 6.20) how on 25 August, the second day of the events, he retired temporarily inland because of some tremors, and

---

[3] Etienne 1998, 29ff.

there he came into contact with the distraught crowds. Pliny, who was eighteen years old at that time, thus watched the catastrophe only from a distance, and could receive no more first-hand information from his uncle. Only much later, in AD 106/7, was he asked to describe the course of events by the historian Tacitus, who wanted to use the account in his *Histories*. An interpretation of the letters must thus take into account that they were written long after the event, and must be seen as a literary work, and not only as a documentary report.

The two letters give extensive information about the characterisation of Pliny the Elder by his nephew, as well as his own self-description. He describes his uncle as eager to learn, and helpful, fearless and courageous. He comforted and calmed his friends in Stabiae with simple explanations 'by repeatedly declaring that these were nothing but bonfires left by the peasants in their terror, or else empty houses on fire in the districts they had abandoned' (*epist.* 6.16, Loeb). While the others stayed awake through the night, Pliny the Elder went calmly to bed, and in the morning tried once more to reason with the terror-stricken inhabitants, who were making ready to flee, but he was overcome by difficulty in breathing and finally suffered a dignified death on the beach. Two days later he was found stretched out and covered up, and apparently uninjured, 'looking more like sleep than death'.

Pliny the Younger in Misenum, too, remained unconcerned, and pursued his daily reading habit. A friend who had come from Spain showed little understanding for this attitude. When the next morning the two left the city because of the earthquakes, they ran into panicky crowds no longer capable of rational behaviour. The Spanish friend too was upset and departed, while Pliny took care of his mother and maintained a stoic quiet and a will to survive. While the masses were wailing and screaming, calling upon the gods or questioning their existence, and rumours were spreading, Pliny remained impassive and awaited his fate. As the smoke thinned, he and his mother returned to Misenum and waited for a message about Pliny the Elder. However, the nephew tells us nothing about conditions in the afflicted area itself.

The biographer Suetonius (*Tit.* 8) informs us that, after the eruption, Emperor Titus (AD 79–81), out of fatherly concern, dispatched a commission of high-ranking senators and former consuls, the *curatores restituendae Campaniae*, who used the possessions of those who had died in the eruption of Vesuvius for the reconstruction of the destroyed cities. However, the residents of the Vesuvius region were not the only focus of interest, for the capital had priority. The major portion of the imperial donations and restoration measures was provided to Rome, which had suffered a fire and an epidemic. The Roman writer Cassius Dio (*c.* AD 150–235) moreover informs us that Titus had inspected the disaster area himself before sending out the aid commission, and helped with available funds, accepting no outside donations (Dio 66.24). Here, too, the emperor appears as the personal saviour and noble donor, in the antique tradition of euergetism (charity), without, however, initiating any comprehensive measures.

The overall view is that precious objects and materials were sought in Campania, and relief actions undertaken for reconstruction. Survivors and refugees were supported locally, to the extent that their settlements were still viable, while the reconstruction of Pompeii and Herculaneum seemed hopeless. Only Stabiae, a nearby villa location, experienced a renaissance, and in AD 120/1 Emperor Hadrian can be credited with the restoration of the road network in the region, particularly the road between Naples, Nuceria and Stabiae (*CIL* x 6939–40). In the third century AD, new construction activity started again on the territory of Herculaneum. The catastrophe thus did indeed have long-term effects. The event was also interpreted religiously in various ways.

The poet Martial, who visited the region of the Gulf of Naples in AD 88, lamented (*epigr.* 4.44):

This is Vesbius [i.e., Vesuvius], green yesterday with viny shades; here had the noble grape loaded the dripping vats; these ridges Bacchus loved more than the hills of Nysa; on this mount of late the Satyrs set afoot their dances; this was the haunt of Venus, more pleasant to her than Lacedaemon; this spot was made glorious by the fame of Hercules. All lies drowned in fire and melancholy ash; even the High Gods could have wished this had not been permitted them. (Loeb)

The poet Statius too held the gods responsible for the incident. Jupiter, he claimed, had torn the mountain out of the earth and lifted it to the stars, only to drop it upon the unfortunate cities (*silv.* 5.3.205–8). Shortly after the catastrophe the Jewish prophetic literature the *Oracula Sibyllina* (4.130–6) held Titus responsible for it, because of his destruction of the temple in Jerusalem in AD 70, calling the eruption divine retribution for his crimes against the Jewish people. Cassius Dio reports that in AD 79 enormous clouds of dust darkened Rome and even reached Africa, Syria and Egypt. In AD 202 he witnessed another, smaller eruption of Vesuvius, which he describes as the work of the giants, the colossal primal figures who had in the legend fought the gods, and were now throwing rocks into the skies (Dio 66.22–3, 77.2). The Christian writer Tertullian of Carthage (*c.* AD 150–230) also interpreted the Vesuvian eruption as a divine judgement to be explained by moral decadence. In an overall defence of Christianity, Tertullian associated the event with worship of a false God or of heathen gods in general (*apol.* 40.8; *pall.* 2.4).

CHAPTER 20

Mining

With the expansion of the Roman Empire and its enormous building activities, the need for raw materials and building materials increased steadily. Their transportation was in some cases carried out over long distances, especially in the case of valuable materials or luxury goods. Marble was obtained not only from Carrara, Italy, and the old Greek centres, but also from Asia Minor and Numidia (Fig. 21), while granite and porphyry came from Egypt. At the same time, with the expansion of their empire, the Romans continued the mining activities of the newly integrated provinces. The demand for iron, which was first mined in Etruria and Elba, and then also at a number of locations outside Italy, was particularly great; some 38 tons of iron were necessary to equip a Roman legion. Moreover, in the second century BC approximately 125 tons of silver coin were already in circulation, a quantity which was to increase more than tenfold very shortly.[1] The increased requirement for lead could be met in Britain (Strab. 4.5.2; Diod. 5.22.1ff., 38.5; Tac. *Agr.* 12.6).

On the Iberian peninsula there was copper (Huelva) and silver (Sierra Morena) in the south-west, gold in the north-west (Las Medulas), and tin in the west; moreover, silver was mined in Cartagena, the Punic New Carthage, during the imperial era (Strab. 3.2.10). Everywhere the Romans expanded the state-owned mines intensively, and dug extensive shafts, up to 250 m deep, with ingenious drainage galleries; scoop wheels and screw pumps (Archimedean screws) were also used for pit drainage. The newly developed gold mines of Las Medulas near Léon were washed out with water brought in by means of numerous aqueducts and redirected river beds (Plin. *nat.* 33.67ff.), which resulted in about fifty extensive terraced open-pit excavation sites.[2]

Wood was needed in large quantities for the smelting of ores; one modern estimate is that some 5,400 ha of forest were felled in the Roman

---

[1] Schneider 1992, 72–3.   [2] Lewis and Jones 1970, 174ff.

Fig. 21 Ancient quarry at Chemtou, Tunisia, with Giallo Antico marble.

Empire every year.[3] Moreover, innumerable tons of slag were created at Rio Tinto and Tharsis, near Huelva, and at Aljustrel, Portugal. Mining left behind numerous barren 'lunar landscapes', as in the Sierra de Cartagena and the Sierra Morena. In antiquity it also endangered the health of the slaves and other workers (Strab. 3.2.8; Lucr. 6.810–15), for lead poisoning was characteristic of the 'pale lead workers' (Vitr. 8.6.11; Sil. 1.231ff.). The contaminated air deposited ever greater amounts of metals in the soil – and not only in Spain;[4] even in the Greenland ice and in lake sediments in southern Sweden increased quantities of lead particles have been found for the time from the second century BC to the second century AD.[5]

Ancient authors, particularly Ovid (*met.* 1.138ff.) and Pliny the Elder (*nat.* 2.158–9, 33.1–6), were already voicing criticism of mining. With pathos they describe how Mother Earth's entrails and veins were torn out, from greed and to satisfy the demand for luxury, so that the ground shook and trembled. Moreover, the exhaustion of these underground resources was, they argued, foreseeable, so that only the renewable

[3] Healey 1978, 152.   [4] Martínez-Cortizas et al. 1999.
[5] Hong et al. 1994, 1996; Renberg et al. 1994.

products of the earth's surface should be used. If the modern idea of sustainability seems to shimmer through here, it still does so against a different background: the analysis may be that humankind is challenging nature, but the conclusion is more moral – an appeal to moderate the quest for luxury – than an environmental call aimed at saving nature (cf. Plin. *nat.* 3.138). Moreover, miners were reported, despite the high price they paid, to have seen themselves as conquerors of nature (33.73).

CHAPTER 21

Urban problems and rural villa construction

HOUSING AND URBAN SANITATION IN ROME

By the end of the republic Rome had grown to a city of almost one million inhabitants. The residential areas of the wealthy were located on the Palatine Hill, which from the time of Tiberius (AD 14–37) was also the site of the imperial palace, and on the Esquiline, Caelius and Viminal hills; the simple people lived on the Aventine Hill and in the lower-lying areas of the Subura, where many craftsmen were also established (Figs. 22 and 23). The *domus*, the private home of the rich citizen, was built in a spacious style, with a high standard of comfort and culture; ideally, it was equipped with a bathroom, 'flush toilets' – albeit flushed by an underfloor channel – and heating. It contrasted with the more modest *insulae*, the housing blocks for the middle and lower classes. There were some 26 *insulae* in Rome for each *domus*; their total number is estimated at 47,000.[1]

An *insula* might be up to ten storeys high, and was generally surrounded by streets on all four sides. Such housing blocks were the objects of speculators, who wanted to squeeze as much profit for as little effort as possible out of them. In the first century BC M. Licinius Crassus ('the rich'), who had made his money during the civil wars under Sulla, was famous as a housing speculator, but other prominent gentlemen, such as Cicero, were engaged in the same business (Plut. *Crass.* 2; Cic. *Att.* 14.9.1). Their profession was a business in which profit was made at the expense of living space and the quality – and safety – of housing. Poor structural quality and cheap building materials, including much wood in the upper storeys, meant great danger. The buildings were often dilapidated, and in danger of fire or simply of collapse, and the cramped conditions meant that escape routes were often unavailable. The tenement houses were often

[1] Brödner 1989, 183.

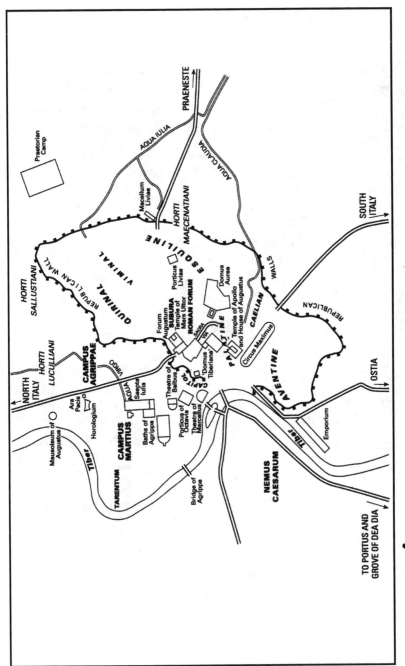

Fig. 22 Map of Rome, c. AD 70.

Fig. 23 Model of ancient Rome: view from the north towards the Subura.

overcrowded, they had no water connections, toilets or kitchens, and the unventilated, unheated rooms provided very unhealthy living conditions, especially when compared with those of a private *domus*. The only heating was provided by coal basins, which filled the rooms with smoke. Water mainly had to be carried in from wells, since only a few flats on the ground floors had their own connections to the public water system.[2]

A sewage system, too, was the privilege of the private homes of the wealthy, so that faeces were commonly collected in pits or bins. Latrines were often located next to the kitchens, and were receptacles for all kinds of waste. Urine was collected by the fullers, who could use it for leather processing. Only those who could afford it visited public toilets, whose number had by imperial times reached 144.[3] From the later part of the first century AD the public thermal baths provided some relief from the miserable residential conditions. They served the purposes of both hygiene and conversation, but used a good deal of firewood, and produced corresponding amounts of smoke.

The streets of the capital were generally overcrowded. Trade and through traffic were constantly in each other's way. The paths of merchants, traders, building carts, litters, children at play and animals crossed in the narrow, winding and unpaved streets. 'In hot haste rushes a contractor with mules and porters; a huge crane is hoisting now a stone and now a beam; mournful funerals jostle massive wagons; this way runs a mad dog; that way rushes a mud-bespattered sow' (Hor. *epist.* 2.2.70ff.; Loeb). The crush of wagon traffic was so great that, by the time of Caesar, it was already necessary within the municipal area to ban such traffic during the day – with the exception of 'rubbish carts' and construction vehicles (*CIL* 1 593 = Tabula Heracleensis, lines 56ff., 66–7). This, however, caused loud rattling and rumbling at night, so that road traffic noise continued at all hours, despite the lack of street lighting (Hor. *epist.* 1.17.7–9; Mart. *epigr.* 4.64.18–24). The poets, too, complained about urban noise – the *strepitus Romae* (Hor. *carm.* 3.29.12; Sen. *epist.* 56.1ff.).

Although residents were allowed neither to dump waste onto the streets nor to throw objects out of their windows (Dig. 9.3, 43.10, 44.7.5.5), and were obliged to keep the streets in front of their houses clear and in repair (*CIL* 1 593, lines 24ff.), much waste lay on the streets (Mart. *epigr.* 5.22). Juvenal (3.268ff.) even warned against going out of the house at night,

---

[2] Carcopino 1992, 55ff. (47ff. in 1939 edn); C. Liedtke, 'Rom und Ostia: Eine Hauptstadt und ihr Hafen', in Hoepfner 1999, 706ff.

[3] Robinson 1992, 119ff.

because of the danger of objects and liquids being dropped onto the street. Although the aediles and a four-man collegium were responsible for keeping order in the streets, there was apparently no regular refuse-collection system.[4] The legal regulations point indirectly to abuses which should be removed. Hygiene was regarded as a communal duty, incumbent upon both the municipal authorities and private persons. Since these measures had to be addressed anew repeatedly, it is obvious that no permanent consciousness of cleanliness ever developed, and waste in residential areas was accepted as a familiar phenomenon. Rubbish pits were therefore located in houses and neighbourhoods, as well as on the outskirts of, or immediately outside, the city, as a number of examples in the provinces also indicate (Vindonissa/Windisch, Carthage).[5]

The air in the capital was of poor quality, even though there were no internal combustion engines. Dirt in the streets, sewage ditches, the vapours of rot and smoke polluted the air. The cremations on the funeral sites (*ustrina*) outside the city exuded additional nasty smells. As early as the first century BC, Horace (*carm.* 3.29.12) mentioned thick smoke (*fumus*) covering the city, and Seneca (*epist.* 104.6) too tried to escape the heavy air of Rome. Even though contagion was in antiquity generally blamed on polluted air (*miasma*) (Hippocr. *flat.* 5), efforts to improve air quality were nowhere to be seen. Even without modern traffic, the ancient city was burdened with considerable environmental problems. Despite the high technical standards achieved in water supply and the sewage system, Rome was still plagued by numerous problems which could never be comprehensively solved.

RURAL VILLA CONSTRUCTION IN ITALY

The upper classes often preferred to leave the city, at least temporarily, to find relief in the countryside from Rome's noise and smoky air (Cic. *ad Q. fr.* 3.1.1; Sen. *epist.* 104.1, 6). The trend toward urbanisation was accompanied by a growing longing for the countryside, where one might try to escape the plagues of the city. Horace (*epist.* 1.14.14ff.) praises the advantages of self-chosen country life, and criticises longings for the city. Juvenal in the early second century AD lamented the inconveniences of the city, but also denounced the pomposity of the rich who could, even in the countryside, enjoy all the amenities of town (Iuv. 3.190–238).

[4] Thüry 2001, 9. [5] Thüry 2001, 31ff.

Since the late republic, the leading families had owned villas in the countryside where they could take refuge after their daily business in the capital, or during holiday stays. A luxurious villa in a lovely landscape outside the city (*villa suburbana*) became an unsurpassable luxury for the upper classes. Prestigious houses appeared which served both for individual relaxation (*otium*) and for maintaining social contacts (Cic. *de orat.* 1.24ff.; Plin. *epist.* 9.36). They were built in the Alban Hills (Tusculum, Lavinium), as well as on the coasts or along the rivers and lakes of Latium, Campania and northern Italy.[6] Moreover, in such places as Tibur, Praeneste and Velitrae, former rustic estates were renovated into splendid villas. Even by Augustan times, according to Strabo (5.4.8), the Gulf of Naples looked like a single city, as a result of the villas lined up in close order along its shores.

P. Cornelius Scipio Africanus the Elder, the victor over Carthage at the battle of Zama in 202 BC, at the end of his career (184 BC) retired to his estate at Liternum in Campania, which was then still simple and well fortified (Liv. 38.52; Sen. *epist.* 86.4–5). Cato too was said to have lived in a simple, unassuming villa in Tusculum (Gell. 13.24). P. Cornelius Scipio Aemilianus Africanus the Younger, the conqueror of Carthage in the Third Punic War, and D. Iunius Brutus planted bigger gardens for their country houses; Scipio apparently resided in Lavernium near Formiae (Cic. *Lael.* 2.7, 7.25; *rep.* 1.14; *fat.* fr. 5). After his retreat to private life in 79 BC, Sulla enjoyed hunting and fishing on his estate in Cumae (App. *civ.* 1.104.488). Cicero and his father had their *villa rustica* in Arpinum rebuilt as a country house (Cic. *leg.* 2.3). With reference to Greek philosophy, copies of entire gymnasia were built for leisure and prestige (Cic. *de orat.* 1.98), and equipped with Greek sculptures (Cic. *Att.* 1.8.2, 9.2). Another villa of Cicero's at Lake Avernus near Cumae was called the 'academy', after Plato's philosophy school (Plin. *nat.* 31.6); at another estate in Tusculum, a part of the garden was also called the 'academy' (Cic. *Tusc.* 3.7; *div.* 1.5.8). Caesar, too, like Marius and Pompey, owned a villa in the area of the spa Baiae near Naples (Sen. *epist.* 51.11).

Pliny the Younger in his letters describes two examples of large, early imperial era estates (*epist.* 2.17, 5.6): his rural estate in Laurentum ('Laurentinum') on the coast of Latium, south of Ostia, 17 miles from the capital, which he would happily visit after the tribulations of a workday, and his villa in Tuscany, at the foot of the Apennines ('Tusci'). Both were equipped with a *xystus* (arcade/terrace) and a

---

[6] D'Arms 1970, 171ff.; Mayer 2005, 59ff.; Marzano 2007, 235ff.

gestatio (avenue/promenade); at Tusci there was also a hippodrome (riding course/gardens). In Tivoli, Emperor Hadrian proudly displayed his position and education in a variegated, natural-style architectural ensemble with an academy, a palaestra, a library, thermal baths and so on, decorated with statues, waterfalls, fountains, nymphs and a grotto. He also had rebuilt on the grounds of his villa such famous buildings and landscapes as the Prytaneum and the Stoa Poicile, a columned hall in Athens, the Vale of Tempe in Thessaly, and the Canopus channel in Egypt connecting the cities of Canopus (modern Abukir) and Alexandria (Hist. Aug. *Hadr.* 26).

The villa gardens were seen as an improved version of nature, and as a statement against its uncontrollability. The urban lifestyle was to be maintained in the countryside too; the goal was to be able to enjoy the same comfort as in Rome. The landscape served as aesthetic scenery. The houses were provided with park-like gardens complete with fountains, pools, grottos, pavilions and sculptures, and separated from the work of the peasantry. Fish ponds, aviaries and animal enclosures (*leporaria, vivaria*), which harked back to the royal *paradeisos* of the Hellenistic east, were also popular. The Roman hunting enclosure was said to have been invented by Q. Fulvius Lippinus in the first century BC (Plin. *nat.* 8.211); at that time, however, the rhetor Q. Hortensius already owned an enclosed and wooded game park in Laurentum (Varr. *rust.* 3.13.2–3).

Horace (*carm.* 2.15) had already denounced the crowding out of farmland by the villas and fish ponds of the rich. Sallust (*Catil.* 13) and Varro (*rust.* 3.3.10) complained about intrusions upon the mountains and the sea. Excessive construction on riverbanks and lake shores was also criticised (Sen. *epist.* 89.21; Sen. *contr.* 5.5); however, these were the usual laments about the *luxuria* of the upper classes. Generally, criticism was levied against one's peers – without displaying any difference in one's own behaviour. The villa owner Cicero, for example, reprimanded fish-pond owners (*piscinarii*) for caring only about their fish, and not about their communities (Cic. *Att.* 1.18.6, 19.6). No further-reaching thoughts about the environment were pursued, nor did any real concept of conservation ever emerge. Statius continued to celebrate villa construction as a victory over the conditions of nature (*silv.* 2.2.4ff., 32–3, 3.1.96ff.).

With the new form of government, the principate, the possibilities for political participation increasingly faded, and had to be compensated for in other ways. By shifting their leisure time (*otium*) to the countryside, members of the upper classes could pretend to uphold the old customs, which were supposedly still alive in the countryside. Neither the emperor nor the senators therefore had any interest in stopping the construction boom. The amenities of villa life were thus maintained until late antiquity.

CHAPTER 22

The environment in Roman Britain

The environmental history of antiquity concerns not only the Greek and Roman world as a whole; local studies, too, are particularly important, and can therefore be applied very well to smaller regions or to single provinces. I would therefore like to conclude this study with a look at Roman Britain, regarding which a number of the topics touched on above have been thoroughly examined, and can be discussed in an exemplary overview.

THE GEOGRAPHIC SPACE

After the first attempts at landings by Caesar in 55 and 54 BC, the island of Britain was already coming under Roman influence, but its conquest did not begin until AD 43 under Emperor Claudius, who occupied large areas of what is today southern and central England and also Wales; it ended in AD 83/4, under Emperor Domitian, when the governor Agricola defeated the north British army at Mons Graupius and declared the line of the Firth of Clyde and the Firth of Forth as the northern boundary of the province. In AD 122, having suppressed a rebellion by the native Brigantes in 118/19, Emperor Hadrian built the so-called Hadrian's Wall between the Tyne and the Solway Firth, with a total length of 118 km. The so-called Antonine Wall, which moved the boundary northward to the Clyde–Forth line for four decades, was built under governor Q. Lollius Urbicus in AD 139, and marked the maximum extent of Roman territory in Britain (Figs. 24 and 25). Further attempts to push deeper into Scotland at the beginning of the third century AD left behind temporary marching camps which can still be seen from the air, but ultimately ended in failure.

Thus, in spite of these periodic thrusts into Scotland, the Romans never occupied the entire island of Britain; nonetheless, even the borders they established in the north constituted two major intrusions

Fig. 24 The principal military installations and main civilian settlements in Roman Britain.

into the landscape. On the one hand, the construction of the walls took advantage of geographical features and a military road built by Agricola between the east and the west coast, the so-called Stanegate. On the other, it also cut through farming areas with no consideration for existing divisions of fields; moreover, tons of turf were cut out for the construction of the wall and its trenches. Furthermore, huge quantities of wood and stone were used, for which purpose adjacent forests to the

Fig. 25 Hadrian's Wall at Housesteads (Vercovicium).

north were clear-cut, and local quarries, such as Barcombe Down near Vindolanda, exploited.[1]

Geographically, Britain is generally divided into a northern highland zone and a southern lowland zone, separated by a line running from the mouth of the Exe in the south-west to the mouth of the Tees in the

[1] Breeze 1993, 73ff., 102ff.; Dark and Dark 1997, 33ff.; Pearson 2006, 16ff., 46ff.

north-east. The highland zone is climatically cooler and wetter, and therefore better suited for livestock raising, while the more fertile lowland zone, with its loam and clay soils, has largely been used for agriculture. However, no strict separation between these two zones is useful here, for one can also identify an intermediate central zone running across the island, which was indeed especially fruitful. At any rate, the Romans profited from a favourable climatic period during the time of their occupation (AD 43–410). Isotopic and botanical data such as tree rings have revealed that the European climate was already getting drier and warmer during the second century BC; then, during the period from 100 BC to AD 250, optimal conditions prevailed overall. As of the middle of the third century AD, the climate in Britain became colder and wetter again, which led to increased flooding. Then, started around AD 400, a major cool spell set in, dropping temperatures by an average of almost 2 degrees and bringing approximately 10 per cent more precipitation.[2]

Accordingly, as of the third century AD, particularly in the southern Fens, the bog landscape around the Wash, flooding increased along the coasts, in part, too, due to the slowly rising sea level. At the same time, there were inland floods on rivers, which carried increased sediments, so that numerous farms had to be abandoned.[3] The causes were both deforestation and erosion, and also poor drainage. Here the agricultural and silvicultural activities intensified by the Romans seem to have had a negative effect in deteriorated climatic conditions; however, this cannot be considered the reason for the fall of Roman rule.

AGRICULTURE, FORESTRY AND INDUSTRY

The Romans had found large areas of fertile arable land in Britain, and also continued to exploit the mineral resources which had already been mined during the Bronze Age, for export to the Mediterranean. Clearing of forestland had already taken place during the Celtic Bronze Age, especially in southern England and Wales, so that the Romans had considerable cultivated land available to them. However, they now undertook additional clearing, particularly in northern England and the area around Hadrian's Wall, and opened up new arable land in higher lying areas, while the forests in eastern Scotland north of the Antonine Wall

---

[2] Jones 1996, 187ff., esp. 197, 220; cf. Lamb 1981; Dark and Dark 1997, 18ff.; Chapter 1, nn. 6–7, above.
[3] Jones 1996, 197ff.; cf. Jones and Mattingly 1990, 7ff.; Pearson 2002, 99ff.

were able to recover and regenerate.[4] Moreover, the Romans improved both agriculture and livestock breeding of various animals, including cattle, pigs and sheep,[5] and introduced new varieties, including the white-fleeced woolly sheep and – a pest – the black rat. Agriculture was improved and expanded in new areas, primarily by drainage and the introduction of the iron mouldboard plough. However, these new areas were increasingly vulnerable as the climate deteriorated, and especially in the highlands became ever less farmable. Around AD 400, clearing was discontinued, and numerous fields abandoned, so that scrub spread, and in some areas the forests could partially recover and expand anew.[6]

During the republican period Britain had been seen as a climatically cold and densely populated country (Diod. 5.21.6), although Caesar (*Gall.* 5.12.6) described the climate as relatively mild. It was famous for its cattle and cereals, which were exported to the Rhine up to late Roman times (Amm. Marc. 18.2.3). Its metal resources too were sought after, particularly tin in Cornwall (Diod. 5.22), and also iron, lead with silver – obtained in open-cast mining – copper and gold; furs, slaves and dogs, too, were exported (Strab. 4.5.2). Tacitus, Agricola's son-in-law in the early second century AD, again described the climate as unpleasant – rainy and foggy, though not extremely cold, so that the soil seemed fertile and suitable for all plants except wine and olives (*Agr.* 12). These were imported, like other Mediterranean foods such as figs and fish sauce, though grapes were occasionally planted in the south of the island (for example, Boxmoor, Hertfordshire). Moreover, new vegetables, such as cabbage, peas and carrots; fruits, such as apples, plums, cherries and walnuts; and flowers, including roses, lilies, violets and poppies, were introduced to the island.[7] The main cereals in Britain became spelt wheat and barley, together with bread wheat, rye and oats, the varieties of which were further improved.[8] All in all, it appears that the food supply and diet were good, as examinations of skeletons also indicate.[9]

In addition to foodstuffs, valuable manufactured goods of glass or ceramics, such as Samian ware (*terra sigillata*) from Gaul, as well as of metal and marble, came to the island. However, the indigenous glass and ceramic production gained increasingly in importance, as shown particularly by the numerous kilns and the mountains of waste in Nene Valley.

---

[4] Dark 1999, 264ff.; 2000, 100ff., 128.
[5] A. Grant, 'Domestic Animals and Their Uses', in Todd 2004, 381.
[6] Jones 1996, 226–7; Dark and Dark 1997, 143–4.
[7] Scullard 1979, 125–6; Alcock 2006, 127–8; van der Veen et al. 2008.
[8] Dark 1999, 264; 2000, 85.
[9] C. Roberts and M. Cox, 'The Human Population: Health and Disease', in Todd 2004, 248ff.

Fig. 26 Main mining areas and products in Roman Britain.

Moreover, salt was panned on the coasts, and coal mined for heating in the central and western regions (Fig. 26). Gold was mined only in Wales, where huge quantities of water were piped in through three aqueducts for the stepped washing areas in Dolaucothi, Carmarthenshire. The local iron-smelting left gigantic slag heaps in the Weald, Sussex, at Weston-under-Penyard (Ariconium), Herefordshire, and in the Forest of Dean in Gloucestershire; they must have caused considerable air and groundwater pollution.[10]

Metals could easily be exported by sea from the southern coast, Cornwall and Wales. There were also many river connections to the interior, which were supplemented by an extensive road network for the exchange both of troops and of goods. Many Roman roadways cut through the landscape on a straight line, and can in some cases still be recognised today. Inns, market towns and small villages were built along the roads and at crossroads. The island was developed anew by improved infrastructure, which also increasingly benefited the balance of trade.

MILITARY CAMPS, CITIES AND VILLAS

The population of Roman Britain is estimated at approximately 3.5 million, including some 50,000 Roman soldiers.[11] They constituted one of the strongest provincial armies, and were established in various legion forts – Caerleon, Chester, York and also Gloucester, Wroxeter and Lincoln – as well as in numerous smaller forts along the coast and in the interior (Fig. 24). They carried out not only military services, but also all kinds of craft work. The settlements and the numerous trades they contained moreover produced a large amount of waste, which polluted the local environment.

A number of new civilian cities also emerged in connection with the Roman forts: with rectangular street grids, public buildings and squares, and water mains and baths, they served both the local market and the Roman administration. The seat of the governor was originally in Camulodunum (Colchester) and was moved during the first century AD to Londinium (London), which, with its approximately 30,000 inhabitants, was the largest city and, with its port, also an economic centre. A total of only four new Roman colonial cities were founded – Camulodunum, Glevum (Gloucester), Lindum (Lincoln) and Eboracum (York) – so that Celtic rural village society, divided into *civitates*, was only partially replaced by urban development. The only already existing settlement or

---

[10] Jones and Mattingly 1990, 179ff.   [11] Jones 1996, 208ff.

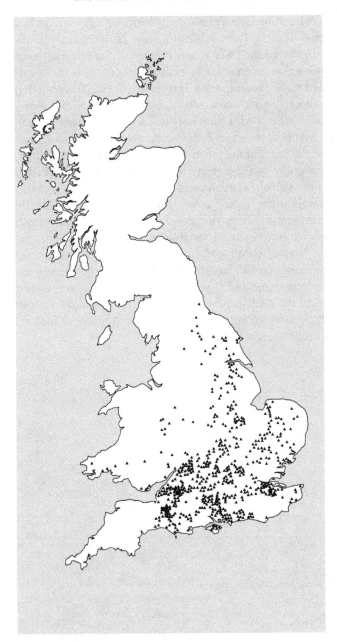

Fig. 27 Distribution of villas in Roman Britain.

Celtic tribal centre (*oppidum*) to explicitly be reported as having been transformed into a Roman *municipium* is Verulamium (St Albans; Fig. 24). In the countryside it was mainly in the lowland zone – except for Wessex – that rectangular Roman villas were next to, or on the ruins of, wooden Celtic roundhouses (Fig. 27), ranging from modest country houses (cottages) with a few rooms in a line, through winged corridor houses, to mansions with three- or four-sided courtyards, which in a few cases, such as that found in Fishbourne, attained palatial dimensions.

Despite the crises of the fourth century AD, Britain was still an attractive target for plunder and settlement for foreign tribes. These included on the one hand the Picts in Scotland and the Scots of Ireland, and on the other the Germanic tribes – the Saxons, Franks and Angles. After the Roman troops were removed from the island in AD 401/2 for the defence of Italy, the fortifications previously established on the southern and eastern coasts, the 'Saxon Shore Forts' (*litus Saxonicum*), were ultimately ineffective. Thus, many Roman facilities crumbled, and the country was used in new – or resurrected old – ways. Nevertheless, the foundations for an urban landscape with a new infrastructure networked nationwide had been laid, from which later epochs were able to profit, despite the damage that had been caused to the environment.

Conclusion

The environmental history of antiquity covers a wide range of fields of analysis of living conditions in ancient Greek and Roman times, and can thus claim relevance for the characterisation of an entire epoch. It shows both continuity of the landscape and changes in the Mediterranean area and the adjacent regions to the north, from the early part of the first millennium BC through late antiquity in the fourth and fifth centuries AD. It leads from the modest beginnings of the world of the *polis* in Greece, which spread across extensive areas around the Mediterranean and Black Seas, to the Roman Empire, with its vast territorial expansion that resulted not only in the conquest of the countries bordering the Mediterranean, but also embraced areas north of the Alps, so that large portions of European territory were opened up to settlement and economic activity. This intensified settlement laid important foundations for the shaping of medieval and hence also of modern Europe. The conceptualisation of nature developed by the Greeks and Romans, and their manner of dealing with their natural environment, would also have after-effects.

A study of the environmental history of antiquity is restricted primarily by the sources, since the literary reports are limited in scope and often provide only a one-sided view of the situation; they can only partially be completed or corrected by the results of natural-scientific investigations. There are no detailed descriptions of the environment, or of environmental problems. Environment in the modern sense was only described at a general level, primarily in terms of such climatic factors as wind and water. Despite the religious respect for nature, it was always seen as a challenge to be mastered and defeated by technical means. Such threatening elements as fires, floods, earthquakes and volcanoes, and also drought and wind storms were to be brought under control. Human destruction of nature, exhaustion of resources and the harmful effects of pollution were noted and criticised, but largely as a critique of opulence, and with no clear analysis of the issues.

Land and resource exploitation had already led to local environmental damage among the Greeks. The impacts of the Romans were of a similar nature, to some extent quantitatively increased; moreover, they covered a greater geographical area. From the outset, the central factors for all regions was agriculture and spreading urban development. Nature was systematically used, without this, however, resulting in any agricultural technological revolution. The soils were over-exploited, forests were clear-cut, river and lakesides built up and obstructed, bodies of water artificially transformed and polluted, animals exploited and harvests destroyed in war. The results, in many places, were environmental damage or soil erosion and decimation of plants and animals. Gardens clearly served the purpose of basic food production, both in the countryside and in the cities and their immediate surroundings, but were also built for their aesthetic qualities, as an element of a luxurious lifestyle. Urban development led to problems of residential hygiene, and made measures against waste, air pollution, noise, fires and traffic necessary. Land parcelling and opening up of large areas of land with roads made it possible for the Romans to build an extensive economic network for the exchange of their goods over long distances. Local specialisation developed, and exogenous plants and animals were introduced in new areas. Roman food products spread across large portions of Europe, although regional differences were still maintained.

The countryside of Europe had changed markedly in many areas, and had both opened up new horizons for people, and also shown them limits of use. Since total populations were still limited, and the extent of overall damage remained relatively slight, or correctable, no comprehensive criticism of the handling of the environment arose. Nevertheless, measures to limit damage and also to protect and preserve resources were indeed initiated by the state. That enabled crops, trees and forests to be restored, albeit often in changed form, and bodies of water and drinking water to be provided to the general public on a long-term basis. Both individuals and the community had to take at least partial responsibility for nature and its assets. Overall, a pragmatic line was pursued, which made nature and its resources available for common use, but also preserved them for the benefit of the community. Nevertheless, the extensive mining of raw materials caused permanent environmental damage, which is in some cases visible or ascertainable even today.

Chronology

Greece

8th century – 500 BC	**Archaic period**
c. 700 BC	Homer, *Iliad, Odyssey*
500–336BC	**Classical period**
336–30 BC	**Hellenistic period**
336–323 BC	Alexander III (the Great) of Macedonia
after 323 BC	Alexander's successors (the diadochi) Hellenistic kingships: Antigonides (Macedonia) to 168 BC Seleucides (Mesopotamia/Syria) to 64 BC Ptolemies (Egypt) to 30 BC
from 146 BC	Roman epoch in Greece

Rome

8th century – 500 BC	**Regal period**
500–30 BC	**Republic**
500–287 BC	Early republic period: Conflict of the Orders
287–133 BC	Middle or classical republic period
133–30 BC	Late republic period: time of crisis
30 BC – AD 300	**Empire**
27 BC – AD 14	Augustus, the first Roman emperor
AD 284–305	Diocletian; tetrarchy
300 – 6th century	**Late antiquity**
306–37	Constantine I (the Great)
395	Division into Eastern and Western Roman empires
476	End of the Western Roman Empire

Further reading

INTRODUCTION

Simmons (1993: p. 153) and Hughes (2006: p. 152) provide introductions to environmental history, with brief research histories.[1] Hughes (1994: p. 154) reports generally on the environment in antiquity; Sallares (2007: p. 154) and Foxhall et al. (2007: p. 154) give a brief introduction. Panessa (1991: p. 154) contains the appropriate literary sources from antiquity. The results of natural-scientific examinations of pollen, tree-ring, ice-core, river and lake sediment, peat, glacier and osteological data – which are published in the respective periodicals, such as *ArchaeoZoologia, Environmental Archaeology, Geoarchaeology, Science, Vegetation History and Archaeobotany* – are also increasingly important.

THE GEOGRAPHIC SPACE

Semple (1931: p. 154) provided an overview of the Mediterranean area in ancient times from an ecological perspective, as do, more recently, Grove and Rackham (2001: p. 154); Horden and Purcell (2000: p. 154) and Hughes (2005: p. 154) do so from a historical perspective. Fundamental for the history of the climate is Lamb (1977: p. 157); the most recent reconstruction based on tree rings is Büntgen et al. (2011: p. 157). The discussion of the deposits in Mediterranean river valleys and their causes started with Vita-Finzi (1969: p. 158), and was continued by Bintliff (1977: p. 156), with more comprehensive examinations. Further individual studies were provided by van Andel and colleagues (van Andel and Zangger, 1990; van Andel et al. 1986, 1990: p. 158) and Brückner (1983, 1986, 1990, 1997: p. 157), who increasingly took human influences into account.

---

[1] Page references in this chapter are to the Bibliography.

PEOPLE AND NATURE

Bernert's article 'Naturgefühl' ('feeling for nature') in Pauly's *Realencyclopädie der classischen Altertumswissenschaft* (1935: p. 158) laid the foundations. Glacken (1967: p. 159) published an epoch-making standard reference. Newer essays on the Greek understanding of nature are contained in Westra and Robinson (1997: p. 159); for Pliny, see Beagon (1992: p. 166).

AGRICULTURE

Isager and Skydsgaard (1992: p. 160) provide an introduction to Greek agriculture; Wells (1992: p. 160) contains select examples. White (1970: p. 168) and Flach (1990: p. 167) wrote important manuals on Roman agricultural history. For the situation in Italy, see Spurr (1986: p. 168) and Jongman (2003: p. 167), who questions the transformation in agriculture, and emphasises the priority of cereals cultivation.

FORESTS AND TIMBER

The pioneering work is Meiggs (1982: p. 161); Thirgood (1981: p. 161) still emphasised deforestation in antiquity. Nenninger (2001: p. 169) and Ulrich (2007: p. 169) provide more current pictures of the Roman world – especially also on timber construction. The most recent and cautious general overview is Harris (2011: p. 160).

GARDENS

The epoch-making general work is by Gothein (1914: p. 161), supplemented by the modern summary by Bonnechere and De Bruyn (1998: p. 161). Carroll-Spillecke (1989: p. 161) and Osborne (1992: p. 161) are comprehensive for the Greek garden; Birge (1982: p. 161) for the sacred groves. The scientific works of Jashemski (1967, 1979 in particular, 1992, 1998: p. 170) are path-breaking on the Roman gardens, using the example of Pompeii. Archaeobotanical and palynological studies which have been carried out for some time at ancient digs, are also important.

ANIMALS

The comprehensive, epoch-making general manual is by Kalof (2007: p. 162). For the human–animal relationship in antiquity, see Gilhus (2006: p. 162). Jennison (1937, with sources: p. 170) provided the basic study on the use of animals in the circus spectacles; Toynbee (1973: p. 171) addressed ancient Rome in general. Archaeozoological studies, which are increasingly being presented in connection with provincial Roman digs, are also important.

FOOD

Dalby (1996: p. 162) provides an overview on Greece; André (1981: p. 171) on Rome. Garnsey (1988, 1999: p. 172) discusses the diet situation in antiquity in general. Davidson (1997: p. 162) gives an outline of Greek dietary habits and physical requirements in their social and political context. Kleberg (1966: p. 172) is the basic work on Roman inns; Carusi (2008: p. 171), on all aspects of salt.

FIRE AND WATER

Crouch (1993: p. 163) is the key work on water supply in Greece; on hydraulic engineering in antiquity, Tölle-Kastenbein (1990: p. 163) and Wikander (2000: p. 164); on Athens, Tölle-Kastenbein (1994: p. 163). On the water supply in Rome and its organisation, Kleijn (2001: p. 173) and Bruun (1991: p. 173) are the basic works. Aldrete (2007: p. 172) is comprehensive for the Tiber floods. Peachin (2004: p. 173) provides an overview on Frontinus and the contemporary water supply.

EARTHQUAKES AND VOLCANOES

Guidoboni (1994: p. 174) offers a summary of the seismic events of antiquity and the early Middle Ages. Waldherr (1997: p. 164) examines the ancient interpretations of earthquakes. Sonnabend (1999: p. 175) and Meißner (2008: p. 164) are the key works on natural disasters and their management.

MINING

Healy (1978: p. 164), Tylecote (1992: p. 165) and Shepherd (1993: p. 165) – and recently also Domergue (2008: p. 164) – provide complete portrayals. Ramin (1977, 199ff.: p. 165) contains the ancient documentary sources. Conophagos (1980: p. 164) and Kalcyk (1982: p. 165) are comprehensive on Laureion. See Davies (1935: p. 175) for the Roman mines generally, Domergue (1990: p. 175) for the situation in Spain, and Penhallurick (1986: p. 165) on tin in south-western England.

URBAN PROBLEMS AND RURAL VILLA CONSTRUCTION

Kolb (1995: p. 177) is comprehensive on the history and design of the city of Rome; Robinson (1992: p. 177) provides a brief summary. Thüry (2001: p. 177) covers the waste problem in antiquity. Hobson (2009: p. 173) presents a comprehensive monograph on latrines. Percival (1976: p. 177) is the key work on villas, along with d'Arms (1970: p. 176) on the Bay of Naples, and Marzano (2007: p. 177) on central Italy, which also contains a detailed catalogue; for Pliny, see Förtsch (1993: p. 176).

THE ENVIRONMENT IN ROMAN BRITAIN

The basic research work was done by Dark and Dark (1997: p. 178) and Dark (2000: p. 178). A useful overview is also provided by Jones (1996, chapter 6, 186ff.: p. 178). More recent overviews of such important topics as 'Health and Disease', 'Economic Structures', 'Rural Settlement in Northern/Southern Britain', 'Domestic Animals', or 'Britain in the Fourth Century' are included in Todd (2004: p. 173). There is an illustrative overview of 'The Economy' in Jones and Mattingly (1990, 179ff.: p. 178). Cool (2006: p. 178) is basic on the question of diet; for the introduction of approximately fifty new plants, see van der Veen et al. (2008: p. 179). An illustrated richly complete portrayal of Roman Britain has been presented by de la Bédoyère (2006: p. 178).

Sources

	De oratore (*de orat.*)
	De re publica (*rep.*)
	Epistulae ad Atticum (*Att.*)
	Epistulae ad Quintum fratrem (*ad Q. fr.*)
	Laelius de amicitia (*Lael.*)
	Tusculanae disputationes (*Tusc.*)
Columella	*De re rustica* (Colum.)
Demosthenes	*Orationes* (Dem.)
Digesta	(Dig.)
Dio Cassius	*Romaike historia* (Dio)
Diodorus	*Bibliotheke* (Diod.)
Diogenes Laertius	*De clarorum philosophorum vitis* (Diog. Laert.)
Dionysius of Halicarnassus	*Antiquitates Romanae* (Dion. Hal.)
Frontinus	*De aquis* (*aqu.*)
Galen	*De alimentorum facultatibus* (*alim. fac.*)
Gellius	*Noctes Atticae* (Gell.)
Herodotus	*Historiae* (Hdt.)
Hesiod	*Erga* (*erg.*)
	Theogonia (*theog.*)
Hippocrates	*De aëre, aquis, locis* (*aër.*)
	De flatibus (*flat.*)
	De morbo sacro (*morb. sacr.*)
	De natura hominis (*nat. hom.*)
	De victu (*vict.*)
Historiae Augustae Scriptores	*Antoninus Pius* (*Antonin.*)
	Avidius Cassius (*Avid.*)
	Gordiani tres (*Gord.*)
	Hadrianus (*Hadr.*)
Homer	*Ilias* (*Il.*)
	Odysseia (*Od.*)
Horace	*Carmina* (*carm.*)
	Epistulae (*epist.*)
	Saturae sive sermones (*sat.*)
Juvenal	*Saturae* (Iuv.)
Livy	*Ab urbe condita* (Liv.)
	Epitome (*epit.*)
Lucan	*De bello civili* (Lucan.)
Lucretius	*De rerum natura* (Lucr.)

Lysias	*Orationes* (Lys.)
Macrobius	*Saturnalia* (*Sat.*)
Martial	*Epigrammaton liber* (*epigr.*)
Ovid	*Metamorphoses* (*met.*)
Pausanias	*Periegesis* (Paus.)
Pindar	*Olympiae* (*Ol.*)
	Pythiae (*Pyth.*)
Plato	*Critias* (*Crit.*)
	Gorgias (*Gorg.*)
	Leges (*leg.*)
	Phaidon (*Phaid.*)
	Timaios (*Tim.*)
Pliny the Elder	*Naturalis historia* (*nat.*)
Pliny the Younger	*Epistulae* (*epist.*)
	Panegyricus (*paneg.*)
Plutarch	*Anthony* (*Ant.*)
	C. Gracchus (*C. Gracch.*)
	Caesar (*Caes.*)
	Cleomenes (*Cleom.*)
	Crassus (*Crass.*)
	Demetrius (*Demetr.*)
	Lycurgus (*Lyc.*)
	Moralia (*mor.*)
	Solon (*Sol.*)
	Themistocles (*Them.*)
	Tib. Gracchus (*Tib. Gracch.*)
Pollux	*Onomastikon* (Poll.)
Polybius	*Historiae* (Polyb.)
Porphyrius	*De abstinentia* (*abst.*)
Sallust	*De coniuratione Catilinae* (*Catil.*)
	Historiae (*hist.*)
Seneca the Elder	*Controversiae* (*contr.*)
Seneca the Younger	*De brevitate vitae* (*brev. vit.*)
	De tranquillitate animi (*tranq.*)
	Epistulae ad Lucilium (*epist.*)
	Naturales quaestiones (*nat.*)
Silius Italicus	*Punica* (Sil.)
Sophocles	*Oidipus Tyrannos* (*Oid. T.*)
Statius	*Silvae* (*silv.*)

Stobaeus	*Florilegium* (Stob.)
Strabo	*Geographika* (Strab.)
Suetonius	*Divus Augustus* (*Aug.*)
	Divus Claudius (*Claud.*)
	Divus Iulius (*Iul.*)
	Divus Titus (*Tit.*)
	Domitianus (*Dom.*)
Tacitus	*Agricola* (*Agr.*)
	Annales (*ann.*)
	Germania (*Germ.*)
	Historiae (*hist.*)
Tertullian	*Apologeticum* (*apol.*)
	De pallio (*pall.*)
Themistius	*Orationes* (*or.*)
Theophrastus	*De causis plantarum* (*caus. plant.*)
	Historia plantarum (*hist. plant.*)
Thucydides	*Historiae* (Thuc.)
Tyrtaeus	*Elegiae* (Tyrt.)
Varro	*Res rustica* (*rust.*)
Vegetius Renatus	*Epitoma rei militaris* (*mil.*)
Velleius Paterculus	*Historia Romana* (Vell.)
Vergil	*Aeneis* (*Aen.*)
	Georgica (*georg.*)
Vitruvius	*De architectura* (Vitr.)
Xenophon	*De vectigalibus* (*vect.*)
	Hellenika (*hell.*)

Bibliography

INTRODUCTION

Terminology

Begon, M., Townsend, C. R. and Harper, J. L. 2006. *Ecology. From Individuals to Ecosystems*, 4th edn. Malden, MA.

Fuchsloch, N. 1996. Einführung in 'Methodenfragen der Umweltgeschichte', in: *Umweltgeschichte. Methoden, Themen, Potentiale*, ed. G. Bayerl, N. Fuchsloch and T. Meyer. Münster and New York, 1–12.

Grobner, U. 2010. *Die Entdeckung der Nachhaltigkeit. Kulturgeschichte eines Begriffs*. Munich.

Hughes, J. D. 2006. *What is Environmental History?* Cambridge and Malden.

Jäger, H. 1994. *Einführung in die Umweltgeschichte*. Darmstadt.

Meißner, B. 2008. Natural Disasters and Solidarity in the Ancient World, in: *Solidarité et assurance. Les sociétés européennes face aux catastrophes (17e–21e s.)*, ed. R. Favier and C. Pfister. Grenoble, 17–35.

Merchant, C. 1993. What is Environmental History?, in: *Major Problems in American Environmental History*, ed. C. Merchant. Lexington, MA, and Toronto, 1–31.

Oliver-Smith, A. and Hoffman, S. M. (eds.) 1999. *The Angry Earth. Disaster in Anthropological Perspective*. New York and London.

Pfister, C. (ed.) 2002. *Am Tag danach. Zur Bewältigung von Naturkatastrophen in der Schweiz 1500–2000*. Bern.

Plate, E. J. and Merz, B. 2001. *Naturkatastrophen. Ursachen – Auswirkungen – Vorsoge*. Stuttgart.

Sieferle, R. P. 2007. Nachhaltigkeit aus umwelthistorischer Perspektive, in: *Nachhaltigkeitsforschung. Perspektiven der Sozial- und Geisteswissenschaften*, ed. R. Kaufmann. Bern, 79–97.

Thommen, L. 2011. Nachhaltigkeit in der Antike? Begriffsgeschichtliche Überlegungen zum Umweltverhalten der Griechen und Römer, in: *Beiträge zum Göttinger Umwelthistorischen Kolloquium 2010–2011*, ed. B. Herrmann. Göttingen, 9–24.

Winiwarter, V. 1994. Umwelt-en. Begrifflichkeit und Problembewusstsein, in: *Umweltbewältigung. Die historische Perspektive*, ed. G. Jaritz and V. Winiwarter. Bielefeld, 130–59.

Modern environmental history: theoretical approaches and periodisation

Bayerl, G., Fuchsloch, N. and Meyer, T. (eds.) 1996. *Umweltgeschichte. Methoden, Themen, Potentiale.* Münster and New York.

Calließ, J., Rüsen, J. and Striegnitz, M. (eds.) 1989. *Mensch und Umwelt in der Geschichte.* Pfaffenweiler.

Delort, R. and Walter, F. 2001. *Histoire de l'environnement européen.* Paris.

Fischer-Kowalski, M. and Haberl, H. 1997. Stoffwechsel und Kolonisierung. Ein universalhistorischer Bogen, in: *Gesellschaftlicher Stoffwechsel und Kolonisierung von Natur. Ein Versuch sozialer Ökologie,* ed. M. Fischer-Kowalski et al. Amsterdam, 25–35.

Herrmann, B. 2009. Umweltgeschichte wozu? Zur Relevanz einer jungen Disziplin, in: *Umweltgeschichte und Umweltzukunft. Zur gesellschaftlichen Relevanz einer jungen Disziplin,* ed. P. Masius et al. Göttingen, 13–50.

Hughes, J. D. 2001. *An Environmental History of the World. Humankind's Changing Role in the Community of Life.* London (reprint London and New York, 2004).

2006. *What Is Environmental History?* Cambridge and Malden.

Jäger, H. 1994. *Einführung in die Umweltgeschichte.* Darmstadt.

Merchant, C. 1993. What is Environmental History?, in: *Major Problems in American Environmental History,* ed. C. Merchant. Lexington, MA, and Toronto, 1–31.

Pfister, C. (ed.) 1995. *Das 1950er Syndrom. Der Weg in die Konsumgesellschaft.* Bern.

1999. *Wetternachhersage. 500 Jahre Klimavariationen und Naturkatastrophen (1496–1995).* Bern.

2002. *Am Tag danach. Zur Bewältigung von Naturkatastrophen in der Schweiz 1500–2000.* Bern.

Sieferle, R. P. 1988. Perspektiven einer historischen Umweltforschung, in: *Fortschritte der Naturzerstörung,* ed. R. P. Sieferle. Frankfurt a.M., 307–76.

1993. Die Grenzen der Umweltgeschichte, *GAIA* 2/1, 8–21.

1995. Naturlandschaft, Kulturlandschaft, Industrielandschaft, in: *Region und Regionalität in der Sozialgeschichte des 20. Jahrhunderts,* ed. W. Bramke and U. Hess. Leipzig, 40–56.

1997. *Rückblick auf die Natur. Eine Geschichte des Menschen und seiner Umwelt.* Munich.

Siemann, W. (ed.) 2003. *Umweltgeschichte. Themen und Perspektiven.* Munich.

Simmons, I. G. 1993. *Environmental History. A Concise Introduction.* Oxford and Cambridge, MA.

1997. *Humanity and Environment. A Cultural Ecology.* Harlow, Essex.

Winiwarter, V. 1994. Umwelt-en. Begrifflichkeit und Problembewusstsein, in: *Umweltbewältigung. Die historische Perspektive,* ed. G. Jaritz and V. Winiwarter. Bielefeld, 130–59.

1998. *Was ist Umweltgeschichte. Ein Überblick.* Vienna.

Winiwarter, V. and Knoll, M. 2007. *Umweltgeschichte. Eine Einführung.* Cologne.

Worster, D. (ed.) 1988. *The Ends of the Earth. Perspectives on Modern Environmental History.* Cambridge (reprint 1994).

Zirnstein, G. 1996. *Ökologie und Umwelt in der Geschichte,* 2nd edn. Marburg.

Ancient environmental history: a review

Blümner, H. 1911. *Die römischen Privataltertümer,* 3rd edn. Munich.

Fedeli, P. 1990. *La natura violata. Ecologia e mondo romano.* Palermo.

Foxhall, L., Jones, M. and Forbes, H. 2007. Human Ecology and the Classical Landscape. Greek and Roman Worlds, in: *Classical Archaeology,* ed. S. E. Alcock and R. Osborne. Malden, MA, 91–117.

Friedlaender, L. 1921–3. *Darstellungen aus der Sittengeschichte Roms in der Zeit von Augustus bis zum Ausgang der Antonine,* 4 vols., 10th edn. Leipzig.

Grove, A. T. and Rackham, O. 2001. *The Nature of Mediterranean Europe. An Ecological History.* New Haven and London.

Harris, W. V. (ed.) 2005. *Rethinking the Mediterranean.* Oxford and New York.

Horden, P. and Purcell, N. 2000. *The Corrupting Sea. A Study of Mediterranean History.* Oxford (reprint 2001).

Hughes, J. D. 1994. *Pan's Travail. Environmental Problems of the Ancient Greeks and Romans.* Baltimore and London.

2005. *The Mediterranean. An Environmental History.* Santa Barbara, CA.

Küster, H. 1995. *Geschichte der Landschaft in Mitteleuropa. Von der Eiszeit bis zur Gegenwart.* Munich.

Marquardt, J. 1886. *Das Privatleben der Römer,* 2 vols., 2nd edn. Leipzig (reprint Darmstadt, 1964).

Meiggs, R. 1982. *Trees and Timber in the Ancient Mediterranean World.* Oxford.

Nissen, H. 1883–1902. *Italische Landeskunde,* 2 vols. Berlin (reprint New York, 1979).

Osborne, R. 1987. *Classical Landscape with Figures. The Ancient Greek City and Its Countryside.* London.

Panessa, G. 1991. *Fonti greche e latine per la storia dell'ambiente e del clima nel mondo greco,* 2 vols. Pisa.

Philippson, A. and Kirsten, E. 1950–9. *Die griechischen Landschaften,* 4 vols. Frankfurt a.M.

Sallares, R. 1991. *The Ecology of the Ancient Greek World.* London.

2007. Ecology, in: *The Cambridge Economic History of the Greco-Roman World,* ed. W. Scheidel, I. Morris and R. Saller. Cambridge, 15–37.

Semple, E. C. 1931. *The Geography of the Mediterranean Region. Its Relation to Ancient History.* New York (reprint 1971).

Sonnabend, H. (ed.) 1999a. *Mensch und Landschaft in der Antike. Lexikon der historischen Geographie.* Stuttgart and Weimar.

1999b. *Naturkatastrophen in der Antike. Wahrnehmung – Deutung – Management.* Stuttgart and Weimar.

Thommen, L. 1992. Raubbau und Umweltprobleme im Altertum, in: *Fernsehen in die Antike. Die Welt von gestern mit den Augen von heute*, ed. R. Surbeck. Basel, 30–2.

Thüry, G. E. 1995. *Die Wurzeln unserer Umweltkrise und die griechisch–römische Antike*. Salzburg.

Vögler, G. 1997. *Öko-Griechen und grüne Römer?* Zürich and Düsseldorf.

Weeber, K.-W. 1990. *Smog über Attika. Umweltverhalten im Altertum*. Zürich and Munich.

Zimmermann, M. 2004. Die antiken Menschen in ihrer natürlichen Umwelt, in: *Oldenbourg Geschichte Lehrbuch. Antike*, ed. E. Wirbelauer. Munich, 121–42.

GREECE

I. THE GEOGRAPHIC SPACE

Gehrke, H.-J. 2007. Die Raumwahrnehmung im archaischen Griechenland, in: *Wahrnehmung und Erfassung geographischer Räume in der Antike*, ed. M. Rathmann. Mainz, 17–30.

Grove, A. T. and Rackham, O. 2001. *The Nature of Mediterranean Europe. An Ecological History*. New Haven and London.

Höhfeld, V. 1993. Landschaftsmuster und Siedlungsanlagen im Yavu-Bergland. Versuch einer systematischen Zuordnung, in: *Die Siedlungskammer von Kyaneai*, ed. F. Kolb. Lykische Studien 1. Bonn, 151–8.

Kolb, F. (ed.) 2004. *Chora und Polis*. Munich.

Osborne, R. 1987. *Classical Landscape with Figures. The Ancient Greek City and Countryside*. Oxford.

Tausend, K. 2006. *Verkehrswege der Argolis. Rekonstruktion und historische Bedeutung*. Stuttgart.

Travlos, J. 1971. *Bildlexikon zur Topographie des antiken Athen*. Tübingen.

Zimmermann, M. 2004. Die antiken Menschen in ihrer natürlichen Umwelt, in: *Oldenbourg Geschichte Lehrbuch. Antike*, ed. E. Wirbelauer. Munich, 121–42.

The era of colonisation

Boardman, J. 1999. *The Greeks Overseas. Their Early Colonies and Trade*, 4th edn. London (reprint 2000).

Dunbabin, T. J. 1948. *The Western Greeks. The History of Sicily and South Italy from the Foundation of the Greek Colonies to 480 B.C.* Oxford (reprint 1968).

Graham, J. 1983. *Colony and Mother City in Ancient Greece*, 2nd edn. Chicago.

Mertens, D. 2006. *Städte und Bauten der Westgriechen. Von der Kolonisationszeit bis zur Krise um 400 vor Christus*. Munich.

Miller, T. 1997. *Die griechische Kolonisation im Spiegel literarischer Zeugnisse*. Tübingen.

Nippel, W. 2003. Griechische Kolonisation. Kontakte mit indigenen Kulturen, Rechtfertigung von Eroberung, Rückwirkungen auf das Mutterland, in: *Aufbruch in neue Welten und Zeiten. Die großen maritimen Expansionsbewegungen der Antike und Frühen Neuzeit im Vergleich,* ed. R. Schulz. Munich, 13–27.

Schaefer, H. 1963. Eigenart und Wesenszüge der griechischen Kolonisation, in: *Probleme der Alten Geschichte. Gesammelte Abhandlungen und Vorträge,* ed. U. Weidemann and W. Schmitthenner. Göttingen, 362–83.

Tsetskhladze, G. R. (ed.) 2006. *Greek Colonisation. An Account of Greek Colonies and Other Settlements Overseas,* vol. 1. Leiden and Boston.

The Hellenistic kingdoms

Billows, R. A. 1995. *Kings and Colonists. Aspects of Macedonian Imperialism.* Leiden.

Cohen, G. M. 1978. *The Seleucid Colonies. Studies in Founding, Administration and Organisation.* Wiesbaden.

Fraser, P. M. 1972. *Ptolemaic Alexandria,* 3 vols. Oxford (reprint 2001).
  1996. *Cities of Alexander the Great.* Oxford.

Grimm, G. 1998. *Alexandria. Die erste Königsstadt der hellenistischen Welt.* Mainz.

Hölbl, G. 1994. *Geschichte des Ptolemäerreiches. Politik, Ideologie und religiöse Kultur von Alexander dem Großen bis zur römischen Eroberung.* Darmstadt (reprint 2004).

Huß, W. 2001. *Ägypten in hellenistischer Zeit, 332–30 v.Chr.* Munich.

Ma, J. 1999. *Antiochos III and the Cities of Western Asia Minor.* Oxford.

Pfrommer, M. 1999. *Alexandria. Im Schatten der Pyramiden.* Mainz.

Weber, G. 2007. Neue Zentralen, Hauptstädte, Residenzen, Paläste und Höfe, in: *Kulturgeschichte des Hellenismus. Von Alexander dem Großen bis Kleopatra,* ed. G. Weber. Stuttgart, 99–117.

Climate, coastlines and estuaries

Barker, G. W. and Hunt, C. O. 1995. Quaternary Valley Floor Erosion and Alluviation in the Biferno Valley, Molise, Italy. The Role of Tectonics, Climate, Sea Level Change, and Human Activity, in: *Mediterranean Quaternary River Environments,* ed. J. Lewin, M. G. Macklin and J. C. Woodward. Rotterdam, 145–57.

Bintliff, J. 1977. *Natural Environment and Human Settlement in Prehistoric Greece,* 2 vols. Oxford.
  1981. Archaeology and the Holocene Evolution of Coastal Plains in the Aegean and Circum-Mediterranean, in: *Environmental Aspects of Coasts and Islands,* ed. D. Brothwell and G. Dimbleby. Oxford, 11–31.

Briand, F. and Maldonado, A. (eds.) 1997. *Transformations and Evolution of the Mediterranean Coastline.* Bulletin de l'Institut océanographique, no. spécial 18. Monaco.

Brice, W. C. (ed.) 1978. *The Environmental History of the Near and Middle East since the Last Ice Age.* London and New York.

Brown, A. G. 1997. *Alluvial Geoarchaeology. Floodplain Archaeology and Environmental Change.* Cambridge.

Brückner, H. 1983. Holozäne Bodenbildungen in den Alluvionen süditalienischer Flüsse, *Zeitschrift für Geomorphologie N.F. Suppl.* 48, 99–116.

1986. Man's Impact on the Evolution of the Physical Environment in the Mediterranean Region in Historical Times, *GeoJournal* 13/1, 7–17.

1990. Changes in the Mediterranean Ecosystem during Antiquity. A Geomorphological Approach As Seen in Two Examples, in: *Man's Role in the Shaping of the Eastern Mediterranean Landscape*, ed. S. Bottema, G. Entjes-Nieborg and W. van Zeist. Rotterdam, 123–37.

1997. Coastal Changes in Western Turkey. Rapid Delta Progradation in Historical Times, in: *Transformations and Evolution of the Mediterranean Coastline*, ed. F. Briand and A. Maldonado, 63–74.

Büdel, J. 1981. *Klima-Geomorphologie*, 2nd edn. Berlin.

Büntgen, U., et al. 2011. 2500 Years of European Climate Variability and Human Susceptibility, *Science* 331, 578–82.

Davidson, D. A. 1980. Erosion in Greece during the First and Second Millennia BC, in: *Timescales in Geomorphology*, ed. R. A. Cullingford, D. A. Davidson and J. Lewin. Chichester, 143–58.

Eumorphopulos, L. 1963. Veränderungen des Golfes von Thessaloniki, *Geographica Helvetica* 18, 269–77.

Fouache, E. and Pavlopoulos, K. (eds.) 2005. *Sea Level Changes in Eastern Mediterranean during Holocene. Indicators and Human Impacts.* Zeitschrift für Geomorophologie Suppl. 137. Berlin and Stuttgart.

Grove, A. T. and Rackham, O. 2001. *The Nature of Mediterranean Europe. An Ecological History.* New Haven and London.

Hearty, P. J. and Dai Pra, G. 1992. The Age and Stratigraphy of Quaternary Coastal Deposits along the Gulf of Taranto (South Italy), *Journal of Coastal Research* 8, 882–905.

Heide, A. 1997. Das Wetter und Klima in der römischen Antike im Westen des Reiches (dissertation), University of Mainz.

Kelletat, D. 1984. *Deltaforschung. Verbreitung, Morphologie, Entstehung und Ökologie von Deltas.* Darmstadt.

Klostermann, J. 2008. Umwelt und Klima Xantens in römischer Zeit, in: *Colonia Ulpia Traiana. Xanten und sein Umland in römischer Zeit*, ed. M. Müller, H.-J. Schalles and N. Zieling. Mainz, 21–30.

Lamb, H. H. 1977. *Climate. Present, Past and Future*, vol. II: *Climatic History and the Future.* London.

1981. Climate from 1000 BC to 1000 AD, in: *The Environment of Man: the Iron Age to the Anglo-Saxon Period*, ed. M. Jones and G. Dimbleby. Oxford, 53–65.

Maise, C. 1998. Archäoklimatologie. Vom Einfluss nacheiszeitlicher Klimavariabilität in der Ur- und Frühgeschichte, *Jahrbuch der Schweizerischen Gesellschaft für Ur- und Frühgeschichte* 81, 197–235.

May, T. 1991. Morphodynamik und Bodenbildungen im westlichen Mittelmeerraum seit dem mittleren Holozän. Anthropogen oder klimatisch gesteuert?, *Geographische Zeitschrift* 79, 212–28.

Nenninger, M. 2001. *Die Römer und der Wald. Untersuchungen zum Umgang mit einem Naturraum am Beispiel der römischen Nordwestprovinzen.* Stuttgart.

Patzelt, G. 1994. Die klimatischen Verhältnisse im südlichen Mitteleuropa zur Römerzeit, in: *Ländliche Besiedlung und Landschaft in den Rhein-Donau-Provinzen des Römischen Reiches*, vol. 1, ed. H. Bender and H. Wolff. Espelkamp, 7–20.

Rackham, O. 1983. Observations on the Historical Ecology of Boeotia, *Annual of the British School at Athens* 78, 291–351.

Reale, O. and Dirmeyer, P. 2000. Modeling the Effects of Vegetation on Mediterranean Climate during the Roman Classical Period: Part I: Climate History and Model Sensitivity; Part II: Model Simulation, *Global and Planetary Change* 25, 163–84 and 185–214.

Schäfer, J. and Simon, W. (eds.) 1981. *Strandverschiebungen in ihrer Bedeutung für Geowissenschaften und Archäologie.* Ruperto Carola Sonderheft. Heidelberg.

Trousset, P. (ed.) 1987. *Déplacements des lignes de rivage en Méditerranée d'après les données de l'archéologie, Aix-en-Provence, 5–7 Sept. 1985.* Paris.

van Andel, T. H., and Zangger, E. 1990. Landscape Stability and Destabilisation in the Prehistory of Greece, in: *Man's Role in the Shaping of the Eastern Mediterranean Landscape*, ed. S. Bottema, G. Entjes-Nieborg and W. van Zeist. Rotterdam, 139–57.

van Andel, T. H., Runnels, C. N. and Pope, K. O. 1986. Five Thousand Years of Land Use and Abuse in the Southern Argolid, Greece, *Hesperia* 55, 103–28.

van Andel, T. H., Zangger, E. and Demitrack, A. 1990. Land Use and Soil Erosion in Prehistoric and Historical Greece, *Journal of Field Archaeology* 17, 379–96.

Vita-Finzi, C. 1969. *The Mediterranean Valleys. Geological Changes in Historical Times.* Cambridge.

Wagstaff, J. M. 1981. Buried Assumptions. Some Problems in the Interpretation of the 'Younger Fill' Raised by Recent Data from Greece, *Journal of Archaeological Science* 8, 247–64.

2. PEOPLE AND NATURE

Bernert, E. 1935. Naturgefühl, in: *Paulys Realencyclopädie der classischen Altertumswissenschaft*, vol. XVI. Stuttgart, 1811–49.

Fairclough, H. R. 1930. *Love of Nature among the Greeks and Romans.* London.

Fedeli, P. 1989. Il rapporto dell'uomo con la natura e l'ambiente – l'antichità vi ha visto un problema?, *Der Altsprachliche Unterricht* 32/3, 32–42.

Fetscher, I. 1988. Lebenssinn und Ehrfurcht vor der Natur in der Antike, in: *Antikes Denken – Moderne Schule. Beiträge zu den antiken Grundlagen unseres Denkens*, ed. H. W. Schmidt and P. Wülfing. Gymnasium Suppl. 9. Heidelberg, 32–50.

Glacken, C. J. 1967. *Traces on the Rhodian Shore. Nature and Culture in Western Thought from Ancient Times to the End of the Eighteenth Century.* Berkeley and Los Angeles (reprint 1990).

Knobloch, E. 1981. Das Naturverständnis der Antike, in: *Naturverständnis und Naturbeherrschung,* ed. F. Rapp. Munich, 10–35.

Longo, O. 1988. Ecologia antica. Il rapporto uomo/ambiente in Grecia, *Aufidus* 6, 3–30.

Mauduit, C. (ed.) 1998. *Paysages et milieux naturels dans la littérature antique.* Lyon.

Panessa, G. 1991. *Fonti greche e latine per la storia dell'ambiente e del clima nel mondo greco,* 2 vols. Pisa.

Sallmann, K. 2001. Der Mensch und 'seine' Natur, *Gymnasium* 108, 485–514.

Sambursky, S. 1965. *Das physikalische Weltbild der Antike.* Zürich and Stuttgart.

Schneider, H. 1993. Natur und technisches Handeln im antiken Griechenland, in: *Naturauffassungen in Philosophie, Wissenschaft, Technik,* vol. 1: *Antike und Mittelalter,* ed. L. Schäfer and E. Ströker. Freiburg and Munich, 107–60.

Siebert, G. (ed.) 1996. *Nature et paysage dans la pensée et l'environnement des civilisations antiques.* Paris.

Sonnabend, H. 1996. Antike Einschätzungen menschlicher Eingriffe in die natürliche Bergwelt, in: *Gebirgsland als Lebensraum. Stuttgarter Kolloquium zur historischen Geographie des Altertums 5, 1993,* ed. E. Olshausen and H. Sonnabend. Amsterdam, 151–60.

Uglione, R. (ed.) 1998. *L'uomo antico e la natura.* Turin.

Vögler, G. 1997. *Öko-Griechen und grüne Römer?* Zürich and Düsseldorf.

 2000. Dachte man in der Antike ökologisch? Mensch und Umwelt im Spiegel antiker Literatur, *Forum Classicum* 4, 241–53.

Westra, L. and Robinson, T. M. (eds.) 1997. *The Greeks and the Environment.* Lanham, New York and Boulder.

3. AGRICULTURE

Austin, M. and Vidal-Naquet, P. 1972. *Economies et sociétés en Grèce ancienne.* Paris.

Brun, J.-P. 2003. *Le vin et l'huile dans la Méditerranée antique. Viticulture, oléiculture et procédés de fabrication.* Paris.

Foxhall, L. 1995. Farming and fighting in ancient Greece, in: *War and Society in the Greek World,* ed. J. Rich and G. Shipley. London and New York, 134–45.

 2007. *Olive Cultivation in Ancient Greece. Seeking the Ancient Economy.* Oxford.

Furley, W. 1990. Natur und Gewalt – die Gewalt der Natur. Zur Rolle der Natur und der Landschaft bei Thukydides, *Ktema* 15, 173–82.

Gallant, T. W. 1982. Agricultural Systems, Land Tenure and the Reforms of Solon, *Annual of the British School at Athens* 77, 111–24.

 1991. *Risk and Survival in Ancient Greece. Reconstructing the Rural Domestic Economy.* Cambridge.

Garnsey, P. 1988. *Famine and Food Supply in the Graeco-Roman World. Responses to Risk and Crisis.* Cambridge.

Goette, H. R. 1993. *Athen – Attika – Megaris.* Cologne.

Hägermann, D. and Schneider, H. 1991. *Propyläen Technikgeschichte,* vol. 1: *Landbau und Handwerk 750 v.Chr.–1000 n.Chr.* Frankfurt a.M. (reprint Berlin, 1997), 82–96.

Hanson, V. D. 1998. *Warfare and Agriculture in Classical Greece,* 2nd edn. Berkeley and Los Angeles.

Hondelmann, W. 2002. *Die Kulturpflanzen der griechisch-römischen Welt. Pflanzliche Ressourcen der Antike.* Berlin and Stuttgart.

Hopper, R. J. 1979. *Trade and Industry in Classical Greece.* London.

Isager, S. and Skydsgaard, J. E. 1992. *Ancient Greek Agriculture. An Introduction.* London and New York.

Jameson, M. H. 1977/8. Agriculture and Slavery in Classical Athens, *Classical Journal* 73, 122–45.

Krasilnikoff, J. A. 2002. Water and Farming in Classical Greece. Evidence, Method and Perspectives, in: *Ancient History Matters. Studies presented to J. E. Skydsgaard,* ed. K. Ascani et al. Rome, 47–62.

Lohmann, H. 1985. Landleben im klassischen Attika. Ergebnisse und Probleme einer archäologischen Landesaufnahme des Demos Atene, *Jahrbuch der Ruhr–Universität Bochum,* 71–96.

  1993. *Atene. Forschungen zu Siedlungs- und Wirtschaftsstruktur des klassischen Attika,* 2 vols. Cologne and Vienna.

Murray, O. 1992. The Ecology and Agrarian History of Ancient Greece, *Opus* 11, 11–23.

Osborne, R. 1987. *Classical Landscape with Figures. The Ancient Greek City and Its Countryside.* London.

Pekáry, T. 1979. *Die Wirtschaft der griechisch-römischen Antike.* Wiesbaden.

Richter, W. 1968. *Die Landwirtschaft im homerischen Zeitalter.* Archaeologia Homerica 2, ch. H. Göttingen.

Sallares, R. 1991. *The Ecology of the Ancient Greek World.* London.

Thommen, L. 2003. *Sparta. Verfassungs- und Sozialgeschichte einer griechischen Polis.* Stuttgart and Weimar.

Thorne, J. A. 2001. Warfare and Agriculture. The Economic Impact of Devastation in Classical Greece, *Greek, Roman, and Byzantine Studies* 42, 225–53.

Wells, B. (ed.) 1992. *Agriculture in Ancient Greece.* Stockholm.

4. FORESTS AND TIMBER

Béal, J.-C. (ed.) 1995. *L'arbre et la forêt. Le bois dans l'Antiquité.* Paris.

Harris, W. V. 2011. Bois et déboisement dans la Méditerranée antique, *Annales. Histoire, Sciences sociales* 66, 105–40.

Hughes, J. D. 1983. How the Ancients Viewed Deforestation, *Journal of Field Archaeology* 10, 437–43.

1994. *Pan's Travail. Environmental Problems of the Ancient Greeks and Romans.* Baltimore and London.

Jahns, S. 1992. Untersuchungen über die holozäne Vegetationsgeschichte von Süddalmatien und Südgriechenland (dissertation), University of Göttingen.

1993. On the Holocene Vegetation History of the Argive Plain (Peloponnese, Southern Greece), *Vegetation History and Archaeobotany* 2, 187–203.

Kaplan, J. O., Krumhardt, K. M. and Zimmermann, N. 2009. The Prehistoric and Preindustrial Deforestation of Europe, *Quaternary Science Reviews* 28, 3016–34.

Kramer, B. 1995. Arborikultur und Holzwirtschaft im griechischen, römischen und byzantinischen Ägypten, *Archiv für Papyrusforschung* 41, 217–31.

Meiggs, R. 1982. *Trees and Timber in the Ancient Mediterranean World.* Oxford.

Nenninger, M. 2001. *Die Römer und der Wald. Untersuchungen zum Umgang mit einem Naturraum am Beispiel der römischen Nordwestprovinzen.* Stuttgart.

Rackham, O. 1990. Ancient Landscapes, in: *The Greek City. From Homer to Alexander*, ed. O. Murray and S. Price. Oxford, 85–111.

Thirgood, J. V. 1981. *Man and the Mediterranean Forest. A History of Resource Depletion.* London.

Wagner-Hasel, B. 1988. Entwaldung in der Antike? Der Mythos vom Goldenen Zeitalter, *Journal für Geschichte* 4, 13–23.

5. GARDENS

Bertholet, F. and Reber, K. (eds.) 2010. *Jardins antiques. Grèce, Gaule, Rome.* Gollion.

Birge, D. E. 1982. Sacred Groves in the Ancient Greek World (dissertation), University of California Berkeley.

Bonnechere, P. and De Bruyn, O. 1998. *L'art et l'âme des jardins. De l'Egypte pharaonique à l'époque contemporaine. Une histoire culturelle de la nature dessinée par l'homme.* Anvers.

Carroll-Spillecke, M. 1989. *Kepos. Der antike griechische Garten.* Munich.

1998. Griechische Gärten, in: *Der Garten von der Antike bis zum Mittelalter*, ed. M. Carroll-Spillecke, 3rd edn. Mainz, 153–75.

Gothein, M. L. 1914. *Geschichte der Gartenkunst*, vol. 1: *Von Ägypten bis zur Renaissance in Italien, Spanien und Portugal.* Jena.

Hoepfner, W. and Schwandner, E.-L. 1994. *Haus und Stadt im klassischen Griechenland*, 2nd edn. Munich.

Nielsen, I. 2001. The Gardens of the Hellenistic Palaces, in: *The Royal Palace. Institution in the First Millennium* BC, ed. I. Nielsen. Arhus, 165–87.

Osborne, R. 1992. Classical Greek Gardens. Between Farm and Paradise, in: *Garden History. Issues, Approaches, Methods. 13th Colloquium on the History of Landscape Architecture*, ed. J. D. Hunt. Washington, DC, 373–91.

Sonne, W. 1996. Hellenistische Herrschaftsgärten, in: *Basileia. Die Paläste der hellenistischen Könige*, ed. W. Hoepfner and G. Brands. Mainz, 136–43.

6. ANIMALS

Benecke, N. 1994. *Der Mensch und seine Haustiere. Die Geschichte einer jahrtausendealten Beziehung.* Stuttgart.

Bouffartigue, J. 2003. Problématiques de l'animal dans l'Antiquité grecque, *Lalies* 23, 131–68.

Dierauer, U. 1977. *Tier und Mensch im Denken der Antike. Studien zur Tierpsychologie, Anthropologie und Ethik.* Amsterdam.

Dinzelbacher, P. (ed.) 2000. *Mensch und Tier in der Geschichte Europas.* Stuttgart.

French, R. 1994. *Ancient Natural History. Histories of Nature.* London and New York (reprint 2004).

Gehrig, U. (ed.) 1983. *Tierbilder aus vier Jahrtausenden. Antiken der Sammlung Mildenberg.* Mainz.

Giebel, M. 2003. *Tiere in der Antike. Von Fabelwesen, Opfertieren und treuen Begleitern.* Darmstadt.

Gilhus, I. S. 2006. *Animals, Gods and Humans. Changing Attitudes to Animals in Greek, Roman and Early Christian Ideas.* London and New York.

Hornung, E. 1967. Die Bedeutung des Tieres im alten Ägypten, *Studium Generale* 20, 69–84.

Hughes, J. D. 1994. *Pan's Travail. Environmental Problems of the Ancient Greeks and Romans.* Baltimore and London.

Kalof, L. (ed.) 2007. *A Cultural History of Animals,* vol. 1: *A Cultural History of Animals in Antiquity.* Oxford and New York.

Lorenz, G. 2000. *Tiere im Leben der alten Kulturen. Schriftlose Kulturen, Alter Orient, Ägypten, Griechenland und Rom.* Vienna.

Mielsch, H. 2005. *Griechische Tiergeschichten in der antiken Kunst.* Mainz a. Rh.

Prieur, J. 1988. *Les animaux sacrés dans l'Antiquité. Art et religion du monde méditerranéen.* Rennes.

Richter, W. 1968. *Die Landwirtschaft im homerischen Zeitalter.* Archaeologia Homerica 2, ch. H. Göttingen.

Sorabji, R. 1993. *Animal Minds and Human Morals. The Origins of the Western Debate.* London and Ithaca, NY, 1995.

Wieczorek, A. and Tellenbach, M. (eds.) 2007. *Pferdestärken. Das Pferd bewegt die Menschheit.* Mainz.

7. FOOD

Dalby, A. 1996. *Siren Feasts. A History of Food and Gastronomy in Greece.* London and New York.

Davidson, J. N. 1997. *Courtesans and Fishcakes. The Consuming Passions of Classical Athens.* London.

Flandrin, J.-L. and Montanari, M. (eds.) 1996. *Histoire de l'alimentation.* Paris.

Gallant, T. W. 1985. *A Fisherman's Tale.* Miscellanea Graeca 7. Gent.

Garland, R. 1998. *Daily Life of the Ancient Greeks.* Westport, CT, and London.

Garnsey, P. 1988. *Famine and Food Supply in the Graeco-Roman World. Responses to Risk and Crisis.* Cambridge.

1998. The Bean. Substance and Symbol, in: *Cities, Peasants and Food in Classical Antiquity*, ed. W. Scheidel. Cambridge, 214–25.

1999. *Food and Society in Classical Antiquity*. Cambridge.

Hopper, R. J. 1979. *Trade and Industry in Classical Greece*. London.

Hüster-Plogmann, H. (ed.) 2006. *Fisch und Fischer aus zwei Jahrtausenden. Eine fischereiwirtschaftliche Zeitreise durch die Nordwestschweiz*. Augst.

Moreno, A. 2007. *Feeding the Democracy. The Athenian Grain Supply in the Fifth and Fourth Centuries* B.C. Oxford.

Murray, O. (ed.) 1990. *Sympotica. A Symposium on the Symposion*. Oxford.

Pazdera, M. 2006. *Getreide für Griechenland. Untersuchungen zu den Ursachen der Versorgungskrisen im Zeitalter Alexanders des Großen und der Diadochen*. Berlin.

Purcell, N. 1995. Eating Fish. The Paradoxes of Seafood, in: *Food in Antiquity*, ed. J. Wilkins et al., 132–49.

Race, G. 1999. *La cucina del mondo classico*. Naples.

Thommen, L. 2003. *Sparta. Verfassungs- und Sozialgeschichte einer griechischen Polis*. Stuttgart and Weimar.

Wilkins, J., Harvey, D. and Dobson, M. (eds.) 1995. *Food in Antiquity*. Exeter (reprint 1999).

8. FIRE AND WATER

Böhme, G. and Böhme, H. 1996. *Feuer, Wasser, Erde, Luft. Eine Kulturgeschichte der Elemente*. Munich.

Böhme, H. 2000. Anthropologie der vier Elemente, in: *Wasser*, ed. B. Busch and L. Förster. Bonn, 17–37.

Bonnin, J. 1984. *L'eau dans l'Antiquité. L'hydraulique avant notre ère*. Paris.

Crouch, D. P. 1993. *Water Management in Ancient Greek Cities*. New York.

Frontinus-Gesellschaft e.v. (ed.) 1991. *Die Wasserversorgung antiker Städte. Geschichte der Wasserversorgung*, vol. II: *Pergamon*, 2nd edn. Mainz.

1994. *Die Wasserversorgung antiker Städte. Geschichte der Wasserversorgung*, vol. III: *Mensch und Wasser*, 2nd edn. Mainz.

Ginouvès, R., Guimier-Sorbets, A.-M., Jouanna, J. and Villard, L. (eds.) 1994. *L'eau, la santé et la maladie dans le monde grec*. Bulletin de correspondance hellénique. Suppl. 28. Paris.

Klaffenbach, G. 1954. *Die Astynomeninschrift von Pergamon*. Abhandlungen der Deutschen Akademie der Wissenschaften zu Berlin, Klasse für Sprachen, Literatur und Kunst 1953, no. 6. Berlin.

Krasilnikoff, J. A. 2002. Water and Farming in Classical Greece. Evidence, Method and Perspectives, in: *Ancient History Matters. Studies presented to J. E. Skydsgaard*, ed. K. Ascani et al. Rome, 47–62.

Parisinou, E. 2000. *The Light of the Gods. The Role of Light in Archaic and Classical Greek Cult*. London.

Tölle-Kastenbein, R. 1990. *Antike Wasserkultur*. Munich.

1994. *Das archaische Wasserleitungsnetz für Athen*. Mainz.

Ulf, C. 2008. Vom Anfang des Kosmos bis zum Menschen. Antike Konzeptionen von Wasserräumen und Wasserformen, in: *Wasser und Raum. Beiträge zu einer Kulturtheorie des Wassers,* ed. D. G. Eibl et al. Göttingen, 143–81.

Wikander, Ö. (ed.) 2000. *Handbook of Ancient Water Technology.* Leiden.

9. EARTHQUAKES AND VOLCANOES

Bianchetti, S. 1998. Der Ausbruch des Ätna und die Erklärungsversuche der Antike, in: *Naturkatastrophen in der antiken Welt. Stuttgarter Kolloquium zur Historischen Geographie des Altertums 6, 1996,* ed. E. Olshausen and H. Sonnabend. Stuttgart, 124–33.

Capelle, W. 1924. Erdbebenforschung, in: *Paulys Realencyclopädie der classischen Altertumswissenschaft, Suppl.* 4, 344–74.

Gilbert, O. 1907. *Die meteorologischen Theorien des griechischen Altertums.* Leipzig.

Helly, B. and Pollino, A. (eds.) 1984. *Tremblements de terre, histoire et archéologie. IVèmes rencontres internationales d'archéologie et d'histoire d'Antibes.* Valbonne.

Meißner, B. 2008. Natural Disasters and Solidarity in the Ancient World, in: *Solidarité et assurance. Les sociétés européennes face aux catastrophes (17e–21e s.),* ed. R. Favier and C. Pfister. Grenoble, 17–35.

Oeser, E. 1992. Historical Earthquake Theories from Aristotle to Kant, in: *Historical Earthquakes in Central Europe,* vol. 1, ed. R. Gutdeutsch et al. Vienna, 11–31.

Rittmann, A. 1981. *Vulkane und ihre Tätigkeit,* 3rd edn. Stuttgart.

Schmincke, H.-U. 2000. *Vulkanismus,* 2nd edn. Darmstadt.

Waldherr, G. 1997. *Erdbeben. Das außergewöhnliche Normale. Zur Rezeption seismischer Aktivitäten in literarischen Quellen vom 4. Jahrhundert v.Chr. bis zum 4. Jahrhundert n.Chr.* Stuttgart.

  1998. Altertumswissenschaften und moderne Katastrophenforschung, in: *Naturkatastrophen in der antiken Welt. Stuttgarter Kolloquium zur Historischen Geographie des Altertums 6, 1996,* ed. E. Olshausen and H. Sonnabend. Stuttgart, 51–64.

10. MINING

Conophagos, C. E. 1980. *Le Laurium antique et la technique grecque de la production de l'argent.* Athens.

Domergue, C. 2008. *Les mines antiques. La production des métaux aux époques grecque et romaine.* Paris.

Hägermann, D. and Schneider, H. 1991. *Propyläen Technikgeschichte,* vol. 1: *Landbau und Handwerk 750 v.Chr.–1000 n.Chr.* Frankfurt a.M. (reprint Berlin, 1997), 97–116.

Healy, J. F. 1978. *Mining and Metallurgy in the Greek and Roman World.* London.

Jones, J. E. 1984. Ancient Athenian Silver Mines, Dressing Floors and Smelting Sites, *Journal of the Historical Metallurgy Society* 18/2, 65–81.

Kalcyk, H. 1982. *Untersuchungen zum attischen Silberbergbau. Gebietsstruktur, Geschichte und Technik.* Frankfurt a.M. and Bern.

1983. Der Silberbergbau von Laureion in Attika, *Antike Welt* 14/3, 12–29.

Meier, S. W. 1995. Blei in der Antike. Bergbau, Verhüttung, Fernhandel (dissertation), Zürich.

Penhallurick, R. D. 1986. *Tin in Antiquity. Its Mining and Trade throughout the Ancient World with Particular Reference to Cornwall.* London.

Ramin, J. 1977. *La technique minière et métallurgique des Anciens.* Brussels.

Rosumek, P. 1982. *Technischer Fortschritt und Rationalisierung im antiken Bergbau.* Bonn.

Schneider, H. 1992. *Einführung in die antike Technikgeschichte.* Darmstadt, 71–95.

Shepherd, R. 1993. *Ancient Mining.* London and New York.

Suhling, L. 1983. *Aufschließen, Gewinnen und Fördern. Geschichte des Bergbaus.* Reinbek bei Hamburg, 38–49.

Tylecote, R. F. 1992. *A History of Metallurgy,* 2nd edn. London.

Wagner, G. A. and G. Weisgerber (eds.) 1985. *Silber, Blei und Gold auf Sifnos. Prähistorische und antike Metallproduktion.* Der Anschnitt Suppl. 3. Bochum.

Weisgerber, G. and Heinrich, G. 1983. Laurion – und kein Ende? Kritische Bemerkungen zum Forschungsstand über eines der bedeutendsten antiken Bergreviere, *Der Anschnitt* 35/6, 190–200.

ROME

II. THE GEOGRAPHIC SPACE

Alcock, S. E. 1989. Roman Imperialism in the Greek Landscape, *Journal of Roman Archaeology* 2, 5–34.

1993. *Graecia Capta: The Landscapes of Roman Greece.* Cambridge.

Chouquer, G. and Favory, F. 1991. *Les paysages de l'Antiquité. Terres et cadastres de l'Orient romain (IVe s. avant J.-C./IIIe s. après J.-C.).* Paris.

Coarelli, F. 2002. *Rom. Ein archäologischer Führer,* 2nd edn. Mainz.

Küster, H. 1995. *Geschichte der Landschaft in Mitteleuropa.* Munich.

Rathmann, M. 2003. *Untersuchungen zu den Reichsstrassen in den westlichen Provinzen des Imperium Romanum.* Mainz.

Strobel, K. 2007. Vom marginalen Grenzraum zum Kernraum Europas. Das römische Heer als Motor der Neustrukturierung historischer Landschaften und Wirtschaftsräume, in: *Impact of Empire,* vol. VI: *The Impact of the Roman Army (200 BC–AD 476),* ed. L. de Blois and E. Lo Cascio. Leiden and Boston, 207–37.

The Roman roads

Bender, H. 1989. Verkehrs- und Transportwesen in der römischen Kaiserzeit, in: *Untersuchungen zu Handel und Verkehr der vor- und frühgeschichtlichen Zeit in Mittel- und Nordeuropa,* vol. V: *Der Verkehr. Verkehrswege, Verkehrsmittel, Organisation,* ed. H. Jankuhn, W. Kimmig and E. Ebel. Göttingen, 108–54.

Casson, L. 1974. *Travel in the Ancient World.* London.

Chevallier, R. 1976. *Roman Roads.* London.

Frei-Stolba, R. (ed.) 2004. *Siedlung und Verkehr im Römischen Reich. Römerstrassen zwischen Herrschaftssicherung und Landschaftsprägung.* Bern.

Giebel, M. 2000. *Reisen in der Antike,* 2nd edn. Düsseldorf and Zürich.

Heinz, W. 1988. Straßen und Brücken im Römischen Reich, *Antike Welt* 19, Sondernummer 2.

2003. *Reisewege der Antike. Unterwegs im Römischen Reich.* Darmstadt.

Herzig, H. E. 1974. Probleme des römischen Straßenwesens. Untersuchungen zu Geschichte und Recht, in: *Aufstieg und Niedergang der Römischen Welt,* II.1, ed. H. Temporini. Berlin and New York, 593–648.

Kolb, A. 2000. *Transport und Nachrichtentransfer im Römischen Reich.* Berlin.

2007. Raumwahrnehmung und Raumerschließung durch römische Straßen, in: *Wahrnehmung und Erfassung geographischer Räume in der Antike,* ed. M. Rathmann. Mainz, 169–80.

Laurence, R. 1999. *The Roads of Roman Italy. Mobility and Cultural Change.* London and New York.

Pekáry, T. 1968. *Untersuchungen zu den römischen Reichsstraßen.* Bonn.

Schneider, H.-C. 1982. *Altstraßenforschung.* Darmstadt.

12. PEOPLE AND NATURE

Beagon, M. 1992. *Roman Nature. The Thought of Pliny the Elder,* Oxford.

Bernert, E. 1935. Naturgefühl, in: *Paulys Realencyclopädie der classischen Altertumswissenschaft,* vol. XVI. Stuttgart, 1849–63.

Fairclough, H. R. 1930. *Love of Nature among the Greeks and Romans.* London.

Fedeli, P. 1989. Il rapporto dell'uomo con la natura e l'ambiente – l'antichità vi ha visto un problema?, *Der Altsprachliche Unterricht* 32/3, 32–42.

Fetscher, I. 1988. Lebenssinn und Ehrfurcht vor der Natur in der Antike, in: *Antikes Denken – Moderne Schule. Beiträge zu den antiken Grundlagen unseres Denkens,* ed. H. W. Schmidt and P. Wülfing. Gymnasium Suppl. 9. Heidelberg, 32–50.

Glacken, C. J. 1967. *Traces on the Rhodian Shore. Nature and Culture in Western Thought from Ancient Times to the End of the Eighteenth Century.* Berkeley and Los Angeles (reprint 1990).

Römer, J. 1981. *Naturästhetik in der frühen römischen Kaiserzeit.* Frankfurt a.M. and Bern.

Sallmann, K. 2001. Der Mensch und 'seine' Natur, *Gymnasium* 108, 485–514.

Siebert, G. (ed.) 1996. *Nature et paysage dans la pensée et l'environnement des civilisations antiques.* Paris.

Sonnabend, H. 1996. Antike Einschätzungen menschlicher Eingriffe in die natürliche Bergwelt, in: *Gebirgsland als Lebensraum. Stuttgarter Kolloquium zur historischen Geographie des Altertums 5, 1993,* ed. E. Olshausen and H. Sonnabend. Amsterdam, 151–60.

Thüry, G. 1993. Natur/Umwelt. Antike, in: *Europäische Mentalitätsgeschichte,* ed. P. Dinzelbacher. Stuttgart, 556–62.

Uglione, R. (ed.) 1998. *L'uomo antico e la natura*. Turin.
Vögler, G. 1997. *Öko-Griechen und grüne Römer?* Zürich and Düsseldorf.
  2000. Dachte man in der Antike ökologisch? Mensch und Umwelt im Spiegel antiker Literatur, *Forum Classicum* 4, 241–53.

13. AGRICULTURE

Astin, A. E. 1978. *Cato the Censor*. Oxford, 240–66.
Barker, G. and Lloyd, J. (eds.) 1991. *Roman Landscapes. Archaeological Survey in the Mediterranean Region*. London.
Bender, H. and Wolff, H. (eds.) 1994. *Ländliche Besiedlung und Landschaft in den Rhein-Donau-Provinzen des Römischen Reiches*, 2 vols. Espelkamp.
Brun, J.-P. 2003. *Le vin et l'huile dans la Méditerranée antique. Viticulture, oléiculture et procédés de fabrication*. Paris.
Diederich, S. 2007. *Römische Agrarhandbücher zwischen Fachwissenschaft, Literatur und Ideologie*. Berlin and New York.
Dohr, H. 1965. Die italischen Gutshöfe nach den Schriften Catos und Varros (dissertation), Cologne.
Drexhage, H.-J., Konen, H. and Ruffing, K. 2002. *Die Wirtschaft des Römischen Reiches (1.–3. Jahrhundert). Eine Einführung*. Berlin.
Ferdière, A. 1988. *Les campagnes en Gaule romaine*, 2 vols. Paris.
Flach, D. 1990. *Römische Agrargeschichte*. Handbuch der Altertumswissenschaft 3, 9. Munich.
Flach, D. (ed.) 2005. *Marcus Porcius Cato. Über den Ackerbau*. Stuttgart.
Flutsch, L., Niffeler, U. and Rossi, F. (eds.) 2002. *SPM. Die Schweiz vom Paläolithikum bis zum Mittelalter*, vol. v: *Römische Zeit*. Basel.
Frenzel, B. 1994. Die Landwirtschaft im eisenzeitlich-römerzeitlichen Mitteleuropa, *Humanistische Bildung* 17, 125–86.
Gummerus, H. 1906. *Der römische Gutsbetrieb als wirtschaftlicher Organismus nach den Werken des Cato, Varro und Columella*. Klio Suppl. 5. Leipzig (reprint Aalen, 1979).
Haas, J. 2006. *Die Umweltkrise des 3. Jahrhunderts n. Chr. im Nordwesten des Imperium Romanum. Interdisziplinäre Studien zu einem Aspekt der allgemeinen Reichskrise im Bereich der beiden Germaniae sowie der Belgica und der Raetia*. Stuttgart.
Haversath, J.-B. 1984. *Die Agrarlandschaft im römischen Deutschland der Kaiserzeit (1.–4. Jh. n.Chr.)*. Passau.
Johne, K.-P. (ed.) 1993. *Gesellschaft und Wirtschaft des Römischen Reiches im 3. Jahrhundert. Studien zu ausgewählten Problemen*. Berlin.
Johne, K.-P., Köhn, J. and Weber, V. 1983. *Die Kolonen in Italien und den westlichen Provinzen des Römischen Reiches. Eine Untersuchung der literarischen, juristischen und epigraphischen Quellen vom 2. Jahrhundert v. u.Z. bis zu den Severern*. Berlin.
Jongman, W. 2003. Slavery and the Growth of Rome. The Transformation of Italy in the Second and First Centuries BCE, in: *Rome the Cosmopolis*, ed. C. Edwards and G. Woolf. Cambridge, 100–22.

Kuhnen, H.-P. and Riemer, E. 1994. *Landwirtschaft der Römerzeit im Römischen Weinkeller Oberriexingen.* Stuttgart.

Lepelley, C. (ed.) 1998. *Rome et l'intégration de l'Empire 44 av. J.-C.–260 ap. J.-C.,* vol. II: *Approches régionales du Haut-Empire romain.* Paris.

Marzano, A. 2007. *Roman Villas in Central Italy. A Social and Economic History.* Leiden and Boston.

Mielsch, H. 1997. *Die römische Villa. Architektur und Lebensform,* 2nd edn. Munich.

Molthagen, J. 1973. Die Durchführung der gracchischen Agrarreform, *Historia* 22, 423–58.

Nenninger, M. 2001. *Die Römer und der Wald. Untersuchungen zum Umgang mit einem Naturraum am Beispiel der römischen Nordwestprovinzen.* Stuttgart.

Oehme, M. 1988. *Die römische Villenwirtschaft. Untersuchungen zu den Agrarschriften Catos und Columellas und ihrer Darstellung bei Niebuhr und Mommsen.* Bonn.

Pekáry, T. 1979. *Die Wirtschaft der griechisch-römischen Antike.* Wiesbaden.

Percival, J. 1976. *The Roman Villa. An Historical Introduction.* London.

Reutti, F. (ed.) 1990. *Die römische Villa.* Wege der Forschung 182. Darmstadt.

Rossiter, J. J. 1978. *Roman Farm Buildings in Italy.* Oxford.

Scheidel, W. 1994. *Grundpacht und Lohnarbeit in der Landwirtschaft des römischen Italien.* Frankfurt a.M.

Schönberger, O. (ed.) 1980. *Marcus Porcius Cato. Vom Landbau.* Munich (reprint 2000).

Schucany, C. 1999. Solothurn und Olten – Zwei Kleinstädte und ihr Hinterland in römischer Zeit, *Archäologie der Schweiz* 23/2, 88–95.

Smith, J. T. 1997. *Roman Villas. A Study in Social Structure.* London and New York.

Spurr, M. S. 1986. *Arable Cultivation in Roman Italy, c. 200* B.C.–*c.* A.D. *100.* London.

Vittinghoff, F. (ed.) 1990. *Handbuch der europäischen Wirtschafts- und Sozialgeschichte,* vol. I: *Europäische Wirtschafts- und Sozialgeschichte in der römischen Kaiserzeit.* Stuttgart.

White, K. D. 1970. *Roman Farming.* London.

Winiwarter, V. 1999. Böden in Agrargesellschaften. Wahrnehmung, Behandlung und Theorie von Cato bis Palladius, in: *Natur-Bilder. Wahrnehmung von Natur und Umwelt in der Geschichte,* ed. R. P. Sieferle and H. Breuninger. Frankfurt and New York, 181–221.

14. FORESTS AND TIMBER

Béal, J.-C. (ed.) 1995. *L'arbre et la forêt. Le bois dans l'Antiquité.* Paris.

Brückner, H. 1986. Man's Impact on the Evolution of the Physical Environment in the Mediterranean Region in Historical Times, *GeoJournal* 13/1, 7–17.

Harris, W. V. 2011. Bois et déboisement dans la Méditerranée antique, *Annales. Histoire, Sciences sociales* 66, 105–40.

Hughes, J. D. 1983. How the Ancients Viewed Deforestation, *Journal of Field Archaeology* 10, 437–43.

Judson, S. 1968. Erosion Rates Near Rome, Italy, *Science* 160, 1444–6.

Kaplan, J. O., Krumhardt, K. M. and Zimmermann, N. 2009. The Prehistoric and Preindustrial Deforestation of Europe, *Quaternary Science Reviews* 28, 3016–34.

Kramer, B. 1995. Arborikultur und Holzwirtschaft im griechischen, römischen und byzantinischen Ägypten, *Archiv für Papyrusforschung* 41, 217–31.

Küster, H. 1994. The Economic Use of Abies Wood As Timber in Central Europe during Roman Times, *Vegetation History and Archaeobotany* 3, 25–32.

Kuhnen, H.-P. (ed.) 1992. *Gestürmt – Geräumt – Vergessen? Der Limesfall und das Ende der Römerherrschaft in Südwestdeutschland.* Stuttgart.

McNeill, J. R. 1992. *The Mountains of the Mediterranean World. An Environmental History.* Cambridge, 72–84.

Meiggs, R. 1982. *Trees and Timber in the Ancient Mediterranean World.* Oxford.

Nenninger, M. 2001. *Die Römer und der Wald. Untersuchungen zum Umgang mit einem Naturraum am Beispiel der römischen Nordwestprovinzen.* Stuttgart.

Petrone, G. 1988. *Locus amoenus/locus horridus: due modi di pensare il bosco, Aufidus* 5, 3–18.

Thirgood, J. V. 1981. *Man and the Mediterranean Forest. A History of Resource Depletion.* London.

Ulrich, R. B. 2007. *Roman Woodworking.* New Haven and London.

Wagner-Hasel, B. 1988. Entwaldung in der Antike? Der Mythos vom Goldenen Zeitalter, *Journal für Geschichte* 4, 13–23.

15. GARDENS

Andreae, B. 1996. *'Am Birnbaum'. Gärten und Parks im antiken Rom, in den Vesuvstädten und in Ostia.* Mainz.

Bertholet, F. and Reber, K. (eds.) 2010. *Jardins antiques. Grèce, Gaule, Rome.* Gollion.

Bonnechere, A. and De Bruyn, O. 1998. *L'art et l'âme des jardins. De l'Egypte pharaonique à l'époque contemporaine. Une histoire culturelle de la nature dessinée par l'homme.* Anvers.

Bowe, P. 2004. *Gardens of the Roman World.* Los Angeles.

Carroll-Spillecke, M. 1994. Römische Gärten, in: *Das Wrack. Der antike Schiffsfund von Mahdia,* ed. G. Hellenkemper Salies, H.-H. von Prittwitz und Gaffron, and G. Bauchhenss, vol. II. Cologne, 901–9.

Ciarallo, A. 1992. *Orti e giardini della antica Pompei.* Naples (English: *Gardens of Pompeii.* Rome, 2000).

Cima, M. and La Rocca, E. (eds.) 1998. *Horti Romani. Atti del Convegno Internazionale. Roma, 4–6 maggio 1995.* Rome.

Farrar, L. 1996. *Gardens of Italy and the Western Provinces of the Roman Empire. From the 4th Century* BC *to the 4th Century* AD. Oxford.

1998. *Ancient Roman Gardens.* Stroud (reprint 2001).

Frass, M. 2006. *Antike römische Gärten. Soziale und wirtschaftliche Funktionen der Horti Romani.* Grazer Beiträge Suppl. 10. Horn and Vienna.

Gieré, A. 1986. Hippodromus und Xystus. Untersuchungen zu römischen Gartenformen (dissertation), Zürich.

Grimal, P. 1969. *Les jardins romains,* 2nd edn. Paris.

Häuber, C. 1994. . . . endlich lebe ich wie ein Mensch. Zu domus, horti und villae in Rom, in: *Das Wrack. Der antike Schiffsfund von Mahdia,* ed. G. Hellenkemper Salies, H.-H. von Prittwitz und Gaffron, and G. Bauchhenss, vol. II. Cologne, 911–26.

Henderson, J. 2004. *The Roman Book of Gardening.* London and New York.

Hondelmann, W. 2002. *Die Kulturpflanzen der griechisch-römischen Welt. Pflanzliche Ressourcen der Antike.* Berlin and Stuttgart.

Jashemski, W. F. 1967. The Caupona of Euxinus at Pompeii, *Archaeology* 20, 37–44.

　1979. *The Gardens of Pompeii, Herculaneum and the Villas Destroyed by Vesuvius.* New Rochelle.

　1992. The Contribution of Archaeology to the Study of Ancient Roman Gardens, in: *Garden History. Issues, Approaches, Methods. 13th Colloquium on the History of Landscape Architecture,* ed. J. D. Hunt. Washington, DC, 5–30.

　1998. Antike römische Gärten in Campanien, in: *Der Garten von der Antike bis zum Mittelalter,* ed. M. Carroll-Spillecke, 3rd edn. Mainz, 177–212.

Pagan, V. E. 2006. *Rome and the Literature of Gardens.* London.

Schneider, K. 1995. *Villa und Natur. Eine Studie zur römischen Oberschichtkultur im letzten vor- und ersten nachchristlichen Jahrhundert.* Munich.

von Stackelberg, K. T. 2009. *The Roman Garden. Space, Sense, and Society.* London and New York.

16. ANIMALS

Andreae, B. 1985. *Die Symbolik der Löwenjagd.* Opladen.

Dierauer, U. 1977. *Tier und Mensch im Denken der Antike. Studien zur Tierpsychologie, Anthropologie und Ethik.* Amsterdam.

Dinzelbacher, P. (ed.) 2000. *Mensch und Tier in der Geschichte Europas.* Stuttgart.

French, R. 1994. *Ancient Natural History. Histories of Nature.* London and New York (reprint 2004).

Gehrig, U. (ed.) 1983. *Tierbilder aus vier Jahrtausenden. Antiken der Sammlung Mildenberg.* Mainz.

Gentili, G. V. 1999. *La villa Romana di Piazza Armerina Palazzo Erculio,* 3 vols. Osimo.

Gilhus, I. S. 2006. *Animals, Gods and Humans. Changing Attitudes to Animals in Greek, Roman and Early Christian Ideas.* London and New York.

Hyland, A. 1990. *Equus: The Horse in the Roman World.* New Haven and London.

Jennison, G. 1937. *Animals for Show and Pleasure in Ancient Rome.* Manchester (reprint Philadelphia, 2005).

Kalof, L. (ed.) 2007. *A Cultural History of Animals*, vol. 1: *A Cultural History of Animals in Antiquity*. Oxford and New York.

Lorenz, G. 2000. *Tiere im Leben der alten Kulturen. Schriftlose Kulturen, Alter Orient, Ägypten, Griechenland und Rom*. Vienna.

Mielsch, H. 2005. *Griechische Tiergeschichten in der antiken Kunst*. Mainz a. Rh.

Peters, J. 1994. Nutztiere in den westlichen Rhein-Donau-Provinzen während der römischen Kaiserzeit, in: *Ländliche Besiedlung und Landschaft in den Rhein-Donau-Provinzen des Römischen Reiches*, vol. II, ed. H. Bender and H. Wolff. Espelkamp, 37–63.

Peters, J. 1998. *Römische Tierhaltung und Tierzucht. Eine Synthese aus archäozoologischer Untersuchung und schriftlich-bildlicher Überlieferung*. Rahden, Westf.

Prieur, J. 1988. *Les animaux sacrés dans l'Antiquité. Art et religion du monde méditerranéen*. Rennes.

Sorabji, R. 1993. *Animal Minds and Human Morals. The Origins of the Western Debate*. London and Ithaca, NY, 1995.

Thüry, G. 1993. Natur/Umwelt. Antike, in: *Europäische Mentalitätsgeschichte*, ed. P. Dinzelbacher. Stuttgart, 556–62.

Toynbee, J. M. C. 1973. *Animals in Roman Life and Art*. London (reprint Baltimore, 1996).

Ville, G. 1981. *La gladiature en Occident des origines à la mort de Domitien*. Rome.

Wieczorek, A. and Tellenbach, M. (eds.) 2007. *Pferdestärken. Das Pferd bewegt die Menschheit*. Mainz.

17. FOOD

André, J. 1981. *L'alimentation et la cuisine à Rome*, 2nd edn. Paris.

Brun, J.-P. 2004. *Archéologie du vin et de l'huile dans l'Empire romain*. Paris.

Carcopino, J. 1992 *Rom. Leben und Kultur in der Kaiserzeit*, 4th edn. Stuttgart (French: *La vie quotidienne à Rome à l'apogée de l'empire*. Paris, 1939; reprint 1990).

Carusi, C. 2008. *Il sale nel mondo greco (VI a.C.–III d.C.). Luoghi di produzione, circolazione commerciale, regimi di sfruttamento nel contesto del Mediterraneo antico*. Bari.

Curtis, R. I. 1991. *Garum and Salsamenta. Production and Commerce in Materia Medica*. Leiden.

Dunbabin, K. M. D. 2003. *The Roman Banquet. Images of Conviviality*. Cambridge.

Erdkamp, P. 2005. *The Grain Market in the Roman Empire. A Social, Political and Economic Study*. Cambridge.

Evans, J. K. 1980. Plebs Rustica. The Peasantry of Classical Italy, *American Journal of Ancient History* 5, 19–47, 134–73.

Fellmeth, U. 2001. *Brot und Politik. Ernährung, Tafelluxus und Hunger im antiken Rom*. Stuttgart and Weimar.

Flandrin, J.-L. and Montanari, M. (eds.) 1996. *Histoire de l'alimentation*. Paris.

Garnsey, P. 1988. *Famine and Food Supply in the Graeco-Roman World. Responses to Risk and Crisis.* Cambridge.

1999. *Food and Society in Classical Antiquity.* Cambridge.

Garnsey, P. and Saller, R. 1987. *The Roman Empire. Economy, Society and Culture.* London.

Gerlach, G. 2001. *Zu Tisch bei den alten Römern. Eine Kulturgeschichte des Essens und Trinkens.* Darmstadt.

Grant, M. 2000. *Galen on Food and Diet.* London and New York.

Holliger, C. 1996. *Culinaria Romana. So assen und tranken die Römer.* Brugg.

Jongman, W. M. 2007. The Early Roman Empire. Consumption, in: *The Cambridge Economic History of the Greco-Roman World,* ed. W. Scheidel, I. Morris and R. Saller. Cambridge, 592–618.

Junkelmann, M. 1997. *Panis militaris. Die Ernährung des römischen Soldaten oder der Grundstoff der Macht,* 2nd edn. Mainz.

Kleberg, T. 1966. *In den Wirtshäusern und Weinstuben des antiken Rom,* 2nd edn. Berlin (French: *Hôtels, restaurants et cabarets dans l'Antiquité romaine.* Uppsala, 1957).

Mattingly, D. J. and Aldrete, G. S. 2000. The Feeding of Imperial Rome. The Mechanics of the Food Supply System, in: *Ancient Rome. The Archaeology of the Eternal City,* ed. J. Coulston and H. Dodge. Oxford, 142–65.

Murray, O. (ed.) 1990. *Sympotica. A Symposium on the Symposion.* Oxford.

Prell, M. 1997. *Armut im antiken Rom. Sozialökonomische Untersuchungen zur Armut im antiken Rom. Von den Gracchen bis zu Kaiser Diokletian.* Stuttgart.

Race, G. 1999. *La cucina del mondo classico.* Naples.

Sahrhage, D. 2002. *Die Schätze Neptuns. Eine Kulturgeschichte der Fischerei im Römischen Reich.* Frankfurt a.M.

Scarpi, P. 2005. *Il senso del cibo. Mondo antico e riflessioni contemporanei.* Palermo.

Schareika, H. 2007. *Weizenbrei und Pfauenzunge. Die alten Römer bitten zu Tisch.* Darmstadt.

Stein-Hölkeskamp, E. 2005. *Das römische Gastmahl. Eine Kulturgeschichte.* Munich.

Thüry, G. E. 2004. Ernährung in der römischen Antike. Der Stand des Wissens und die 'kulinarische Rekonstruktion', *Gymnasium* 111, 25–42.

von Ungern-Sternberg, J. 1991. Die politische und soziale Bedeutung der spätrepublikanischen leges frumentariae, in: *Nourrir la plèbe,* ed. A. Giovannini. Basel and Kassel, 19–41 (reprinted in J. von Ungern-Sternberg, *Römische Studien,* Munich and Leipzig, 2006, 287–305).

Wilkins, J., Harvey, D. and Dobson, M. (eds.) 1995. *Food in Antiquity.* Exeter (reprint 1999).

18. FIRE AND WATER

Aldrete, G. S. 2007. *Floods of the Tiber in Ancient Rome.* Baltimore.

Becher, I. 1985. Tiberüberschwemmungen. Die Interpretation von Prodigien in Augusteischer Zeit, *Klio* 67, 471–9.

Bonnin, J. 1984. *L'eau dans l'Antiquité. L'hydraulique avant notre ère.* Paris.

Bruun, C. 1991. *The Water Supply of Ancient Rome. A Study of Roman Imperial Administration.* Commentationes Humanarum Litterarum 93. Helsinki.

Dietrich, W. 1986. *Wasser für das antike Rom.* Berlin.

Dodge, H. 2000. 'Greater than the Pyramids'. The Water Supply of Ancient Rome, in: *Ancient Rome. The Archaeology of the Eternal City,* ed. J. Coulston and H. Dodge. Oxford, 166–209.

Drasch, G. A. 1982. Lead Burden in Prehistorical, Historical and Modern Human Bones, *Science of Total Environment* 24, 199–231.

Eck, W. 2008. Landwirtschaftliche Bewässerung in römischer Zeit in ariden Gebieten nach schriftlichen Quellen, in: *Cura Aquarum in Jordanien,* ed. C. Ohlig. Siegburg, 227–38.

Eschebach, H. 1979. Die Gebrauchswasserversorgung des antiken Pompeji, *Antike Welt* 10/2, 3–24.

Evans, H. B. 1982. Agrippa's Water Plan, *American Journal of Archaeology* 86, 401–11.

Frontinus-Gesellschaft e.v. (ed.) 1989. *Die Wasserversorgung antiker Städte. Geschichte der Wasserversorgung,* vol. I: *Wasserversorgung im antiken Rom,* 4th edn. Mainz.

1991. *Die Wasserversorgung antiker Städte. Geschichte der Wasserversorgung,* vol. II: *Pergamon,* 2nd edn. Mainz.

1994. *Die Wasserversorgung antiker Städte. Geschichte der Wasserversorgung,* vol. III: *Mensch und Wasser,* 2nd edn. Mainz.

Garbrecht, G. 1984. Die antiken Wasserleitungen Roms, *Antike Welt* 15/2, 2–13.

Geißler, K. 1998. *Die öffentliche Wasserversorgung im römischen Recht.* Freiburger Rechtsgeschichtliche Abhandlungen N.F. 29. Berlin.

Haan, N. de and Jansen, G. C. M. (eds.) 1996. *Cura Aquarum in Campania.* Bulletin Antieke Beschaving Suppl. 4. Leiden.

Hobson, B. 2009. *Latrinae et Foricae. Toilets in the Roman World.* London.

Hodge, A. T. 1992. *Roman Aqueducts & Water Supply.* London.

Hüster-Plogmann, H. (ed.) 2006. *Fisch und Fischer aus zwei Jahrtausenden. Eine fischereiwirtschaftliche Zeitreise durch die Nordwestschweiz.* Augst.

Jansen, G. C. M. (ed.) 2001. *Cura Aquarum in Sicilia.* Bulletin Antieke Beschaving Suppl. 6. Leiden.

Kleijn, G. de 2001. *The Water Supply of Ancient Rome. City Area, Water, and Population.* Amsterdam.

Kolb, F. 1995. *Rom. Die Geschichte der Stadt in der Antike.* Munich, 539–50.

Le Gall, J. 1952. Le Tibre. Fleuve de Rome dans l'Antiquité (dissertation), Paris.

Malissard, A. 1994. *Les Romains et l'eau. Fontaines, salles de bain, thermes, égouts, aqueducs.* Paris.

Nriagu, J. O. 1983. *Lead and Lead Poisoning in Antiquity.* New York and Chichester.

Peachin, M. 2004. *Frontinus and the Curae of the Curator Aquarum.* Stuttgart.

Robinson, O. F. 1980. The Water Supply of Rome, *Studia et Documenta Historiae et Iuris* 46, 44–86.

1992. *Ancient Rome. City Planning and Administration.* London and New York.

Schnitter, N. 1978. Römische Talsperren, *Antike Welt* 9/2, 25–32.

1994. *A History of Dams. The Useful Pyramids.* Rotterdam and Brookfield.

Scobie, A. 1986. Slums, Sanitation and Morality in the Roman World, *Klio* 68, 399–433.

Technische Universität Braunschweig 1992. *Geschichte der Wasserwirtschaft und des Wasserbaus im mediterranen Raum.* Mitteilungen des Leichtweiss-Instituts für Wasserbau der Technischen Universität Braunschweig 117. Brunswick.

Thomas, R. and Wilson, A. 1994. Water Supply for Roman Farms in Latium and Southern Etruria, *Papers of the British School at Rome* 62, 139–96.

Thüry, G. E. 2001. *Müll und Marmorsäulen. Siedlungshygiene in der römischen Antike.* Mainz.

Tölle-Kastenbein, R. 1990. *Antike Wasserkultur.* Munich.

Weeber, K.-W. 1990. *Smog über Attika. Umweltverhalten im Altertum.* Zürich and Munich, 169–90.

Werner, D. 1986a. Rom, die wasserreichste Stadt des Altertums. Bemerkungen aus bautechnischer Sicht, *Das Altertum* 32, 36–42.

1986b. *Wasser für das antike Rom.* Berlin.

Wikander, Ö. (ed.) 2000. *Handbook of Ancient Water Technology.* Leiden.

Wiplinger, G. (ed.) 2006. *Cura Aquarum in Ephesus.* Bulletin Antieke Beschaving Suppl. 12, 2 vols. Leiden.

19. EARTHQUAKES AND VOLCANOES

Albore Livadie, C. (ed.) 1986. *Tremblements de terre, éruptions volcaniques et vie des hommes dans la Campanie antique.* Naples.

Bonz-Ammon, D., Reinhart, G. and Schirok, E. 1994. *Studienfahrt an den Golf von Neapel. Vesuv, Pompeji, Herculaneum.* Basel.

Cooley, A. E. and Cooley, M. G. L. 2004. *Pompeii. A Sourcebook.* London and New York (reprint 2007).

Eigler, U. 2005. *Der Vesuv von 79 bis 1979 – Nachbeben in Literatur, Malerei und Film von Plinius bis Wolfgang Held.* Dialog Schule – Wissenschaft, Klassische Sprachen und Literaturen 39. Munich, 71–96.

Etienne, R. 1998. *Pompeji. Das Leben in einer antiken Stadt,* 5th edn. Stuttgart (French: *La vie quotidienne à Pompéi.* Paris, 1966).

Franchi dell'Orto, L. (ed.) 1993. *Ercolano 1738–1988. 250 anni di ricercha archeologica.* Rome.

Guidoboni, E. 1994. *Catalogue of Ancient Earthquakes in the Mediterranean Area up to the 10th Century.* Rome.

Guzzo, P. G. and Wieczorek, A. (eds.) 2004. *Pompeji. Die Stunden des Untergangs. 24. August 79 n.Chr.* [Exhibition catalogue, Mannheim]. Darmstadt.

Jones, N. F. 2001. Pliny the Younger's Vesuvius Letters (6.16 and 6.20), *Classical World* 95, 31–48.

Krafft, M. 1993. *Vulkane, Feuer der Erde. Die Geschichte der Vulkanologie.* Ravensburg (French: *Les feux de la terre. Histoire des volcans.* Paris, 1991; reprint 2003).

Nazzaro, A. 1997. *Il Vesuvio. Storia eruttiva e teorie vulcanologiche.* Naples.

Preusse, E. 1934. Ein Wort zur Vesuvgestalt und Vesuvtätigkeit im Altertum, *Klio* 27, 295–310.

Renna, E. 1992. *Vesuvius Mons. Aspetti del Vesuvio nel mondo antico. Tra filologia archeologia vulcanologia.* Naples.

Santacroce, R. (ed.) 1987. *Somma-Vesuvius.* Rome.

Scandone, R., Giacomellia, L. and Gasparinia, P. 1993. Mount Vesuvius. 2000 Years of Volcanological Observations, *Journal of Volcanology and Geothermal Research* 58, 5–25.

Sigurdsson, H. 1999. *Melting Earth. The History of Ideas on Volcanic Eruptions.* Oxford.

Sigurdsson, H., Carey, S., Cornell, W. and Pescatore, T. 1985. The Eruption of Vesuvius in A.D. 79, *National Geographic Research* 1/3, 332–87.

Sonnabend, H. 1999. *Naturkatastrophen in der Antike. Wahrnehmung – Deutung – Management.* Stuttgart and Weimar.

Waldherr, G. 1997. *Erdbeben. Das außergewöhnliche Normale. Zur Rezeption seismischer Aktivitäten in literarischen Quellen vom 4. Jahrhundert v.Chr. bis zum 4. Jahrhundert n.Chr.* Stuttgart.

Waldherr, G. H. and Smolka, A. (eds.) 2007. *Antike Erdbeben im alpinen und zirkumalpinen Raum/Earthquakes in Antiquity in the Alpine and Circum-Alpine Region.* Stuttgart.

20. MINING

Davies, O. 1935. *Roman Mines in Europe.* Oxford (reprint New York, 1979).

Domergue, C. 1990. *Les mines de la Péninsule ibérique dans l'Antiquité romaine.* Rome. 2008. *Les mines antiques. La production des métaux aux époques grecque et romaine.* Paris.

Healy, J. F. 1978. *Mining and Metallurgy in the Greek and Roman World.* London.

Hong, S., Candelone, J.-P., Patterson, C. C. and Boutron, C. F. 1994. Greenland Ice Evidence of Hemispheric Lead Pollution Two Millennia Ago by Greek and Roman Civilizations, *Science* 265, 1841–3.

1996. History of Ancient Copper Smelting Pollution during Roman and Medieval Times Recorded in Greenland Ice, *Science* 272, 246–9.

Jones, G. D. B. 1980. The Roman Mines at Riotinto, *Journal of Roman Studies* 70, 146–65.

Jones, R. F. J. and Bird, D. G. 1972. Roman Gold-Mining in North-West Spain, II. Workings on the Rio Duerna, *Journal of Roman Studies* 62, 59–74.

Lewis, P. R. and Jones, G. D. B. 1970. Roman Gold-Mining in North-West Spain, *Journal of Roman Studies* 60, 169–85.

Martínez-Cortizas, A., Pontevedra-Pombal, X., García-Rodeja, E., Nóvoa-Muñoz, J. C. and Shotyk, W. 1999. Mercury in a Spanish Peat Bog.

Archive of Climate Change and Atmospheric Metal Deposition, *Science* 284, 939–42.

Meier, S. W. 1995. Blei in der Antike. Bergbau, Verhüttung, Fernhandel (dissertation), Zürich.

Ramin, J. 1977. *La technique minière et métallurgique des Anciens.* Brussels.

Renberg, I., Wik Persson, M. and Emteryd, O. 1994. Pre-industrial Atmospheric Lead Contamination Detected in Swedish Lake Sediments, *Nature* 368, 323–6.

Rosumek, P. 1982. *Technischer Fortschritt und Rationalisierung im antiken Bergbau.* Bonn.

Schneider, H. 1992. *Einführung in die antike Technikgeschichte.* Darmstadt, 71–95.

Shepherd, R. 1993. *Ancient Mining.* London and New York.

Suhling, L. 1983. *Aufschließen, Gewinnen und Fördern. Geschichte des Bergbaus.* Reinbek bei Hamburg, 49–67.

Tylecote, R. F. 1992. *A History of Metallurgy*, 2nd edn. London.

Wertime, T. A. 1983. The Furnace versus the Goat. The Pyrotechnologic Industries and Mediterranean Deforestation in Antiquity, *Journal of Field Archaeology* 10/4, 445–52.

21. URBAN PROBLEMS AND RURAL VILLA CONSTRUCTION

Ballet, P., Cordier, P. and Monteil, M. (eds.) 2003. *La ville et ses déchets dans le monde romain. Rebuts et recyclages.* Montagnac.

Brödner, E. 1989. *Wohnen in der Antike.* Darmstadt.

Carcopino, J. 1992. *Rom. Leben und Kultur in der Kaiserzeit,* 4th edn. Stuttgart (French: *La vie quotidienne à Rome à l'apogée de l'empire.* Paris, 1939; reprint 1990).

Coulston, J. and Dodge, H. (eds.) 2000. *Ancient Rome. The Archaeology of the Eternal City.* Oxford.

Dahlmann, H. 1978. Über den Lärm, *Gymnasium* 85, 206–27.

D'Arms, J. H. 1970. *Romans on the Bay of Naples. A Social and Cultural Study of the Villas and Their Owners from 150 B.C. to A.D. 400.* London.

Eck, W. 2008. Verkehr und Verkehrsregeln in einer antiken Großstadt. Das Beispiel Rom, in: *Stadtverkehr in der antiken Welt,* ed. D. Mertens. Wiesbaden, 59–69.

Förtsch, R. 1993. *Archäologischer Kommentar zu den Villenbriefen des jüngeren Plinius.* Mainz.

Hoepfner, W. (ed.) 1999. *Geschichte des Wohnens,* vol. 1: *5000 v.–500 n.Chr. Vorgeschichte, Frühgeschichte, Antike.* Stuttgart.

Hösel, G. 1990. *Unser Abfall aller Zeiten. Eine Kulturgeschichte der Städtereinigung,* 2nd edn. Munich.

Hope, V. M. and Marshall, E. (eds.) 2000. *Death and Disease in the Ancient City.* London and New York.

Jansen, G. C. M. 2000. Systems for the Disposal of Waste and Excreta in Roman Cities. The Situation in Pompeii, Herculaneum and Ostia, in: *Sordes urbis.*

La eliminación de residuos en la ciudad romana, ed. X. Dupré Raventós and J.-A. Remolà. Rome, 37–49.

Kolb, F. 1995. *Rom. Die Geschichte der Stadt in der Antike.* Munich.

Kunst, C. 2008. *Leben und Wohnen in der römischen Stadt,* 2nd edn. Darmstadt.

Liebeschuetz, W. 2000. Rubbish disposal in Greek and Roman cities, in: *Sordes urbis. La eliminación de residuos en la ciudad romana,* ed. X. Dupré Raventós and J.-A. Remolà. Rome, 51–61.

Marzano, A. 2007. *Roman Villas in Central Italy. A Social and Economic History.* Leiden and Boston.

Mayer, J. W. 2005. *Imus ad villam. Studien zur Villeggiatur im stadtrömischen Suburbium in der späten Republik und frühen Kaiserzeit.* Geographica Historica 20. Stuttgart.

Mielsch, H. 1997. *Die römische Villa. Architektur und Lebensform,* 2nd edn. Munich.

Neudecker, R. 1994. *Die Pracht der Latrine. Zum Wandel öffentlicher Bedürfnisanstalten in der kaiserzeitlichen Stadt.* Munich.

Panciera, S. 2000. Nettezza urbana a Roma. Organizzazione e responsabili, in: *Sordes urbis. La eliminación de residuos en la ciudad romana,* ed. X. Dupré Raventós and J.-A. Remolà. Rome, 95–105.

Percival, J. 1976. *The Roman Villa. An Historical Introduction.* London.

Reutti, F. (ed.) 1990. *Die römische Villa.* Wege der Forschung 182. Darmstadt.

Robinson, O. F. 1992. *Ancient Rome. City Planning and Administration.* London and New York.

Schneider, K. 1995. *Villa und Natur. Eine Studie zur römischen Oberschichtskultur im letzten vor- und ersten nachchristlichen Jahrhundert.* Munich.

Sonnabend, H. 1992. Stadtverkehr im antiken Rom. Probleme und Lösungsversuche, *Die alte Stadt* 19, 183–94.

Thüry, G. E. 2001. *Müll und Marmorsäulen. Siedlungshygiene in der römischen Antike.* Mainz.

2003. Müll und die römische Stadt, in: *Müll. Facetten von der Steinzeit bis zum Gelben Sack,* ed. M. Fansa and S. Wolfram. Mainz, 67–74.

Weeber, K.-W. 1997. *Alltag im Alten Rom. Das Leben in der Stadt. Ein Lexikon,* 6th edn. Düsseldorf.

22. THE ENVIRONMENT IN ROMAN BRITAIN

Alcock, J. P. 2001. *Food in Roman Britain.* Stroud.

2006. *Life in Roman Britain,* Stroud (reprint of *English Heritage Book of Life in Roman Britain,* London, 1996).

Allason-Jones, L. 2008. *Daily Life in Roman Britain.* Oxford.

Arnold, C. J. 1984. *Roman Britain to Saxon England. An Archaeological Study.* London and Sydney.

Bidwell, P. 1997. *English Heritage Book of Roman Forts in Britain.* London (reprint 2002).

Breeze, D. J. 1993. *The Northern Frontiers of Roman Britain.* London (reprint of 1982 edn).

Breeze, D. J. and Dobson, B. 1987. *Hadrian's Wall*, 3rd edn. London (reprint 1991).

Burgers, A. 2001. *The Water Supplies and Related Structures of Roman Britain.* Oxford.

Burnham, B. C. and Wacher, J. 1990. *The 'Small Towns' of Roman Britain.* London.

Capelle, T. 1990. *Archäologie der Angelsachsen. Eigenständigkeit und kontinentale Bindung vom 5. bis 9. Jahrhundert.* Darmstadt.

Clayton, P. A. (ed.) 1980. *A Companion to Roman Britain.* Oxford.

Cool, H. E. M. 2006. *Eating and Drinking in Roman Britain.* Cambridge.

Dark, K. R. 1994. *Civitas to Kingdom. British Political Continuity, 300–800.* London.

Dark, K. and Dark, P. 1997. *The Landscape of Roman Britain.* Phoenix Mill.

Dark, P. 1999. Pollen Evidence for the Environment of Roman Britain, *Britannia* 30, 247–72.

2000. *The Environment of Britain in the First Millennium* A.D. London.

Davies, H. 2002. *Roads in Roman Britain.* Stroud.

de la Bédoyère, G. 1991. *The Buildings of Roman Britain.* London.

1993. *English Heritage Book of Roman Villas and the Countryside.* London.

2003. *Roman Towns in Britain.* Stroud (reprint 2004).

2006. *Roman Britain. A New History.* London.

Esmonde Cleary, A. S. 1989. *The Ending of Roman Britain.* London (reprint 1991).

Frere, S. 1992. *Britannia. A History of Roman Britain*, 3rd edn. London.

Hanley, R. 1987. *Villages in Roman Britain.* Aylesbury. (2nd edn: Princes Risborough, 2000).

Hanson, W. S. and Maxwell, G. S. 1983. *Rome's North-West Frontier. The Antonine Wall.* Edinburgh.

Higham, N. 1992. *Rome, Britain and the Anglo-Saxons.* London.

Hingley, R. 1989. *Rural Settlement in Roman Britain.* London.

Isserlin, R. 2001. *Towns and Power in Roman Britain.* Stroud.

Johnson, S. 1980. *Later Roman Britain.* London.

Jones, B. and Mattingly, D. 1990. *An Atlas of Roman Britain.* Oxford (reprint 2002).

Jones, M. E. 1996. *The End of Roman Britain.* Ithaca and London.

Jones, R. F. J. 1991. *Britain in the Roman Period. Recent Trends.* Sheffield.

Lamb, H. H. 1981. Climate from 1000 BC to 1000 AD, in: *The Environment of Man. The Iron Age to the Anglo-Saxon Period*, ed. M. Jones and G. Dimbleby. Oxford, 53–65.

Macklin, M. G. and Lewin, J. 1993. Holocene River Alluviation in Britain, in: *Geomorphology and Geoecology. Fluvial Geomorphology*, ed. I. Douglas and J. Hagedorn. Zeitschrift für Geomorphologie Suppl. 88. Berlin and Stuttgart, 109–22.

MacMahon, A. 2003. *The Taberna Structures of Roman Britain.* Oxford.

Marsden, P. 1980. *Roman London.* London.

Mattingly, D. 2006. *An Imperial Possession. Britain in the Roman Empire, 54 BC–AD 409*. London.

Merrifield, R. 1983. *London. City of the Romans*. London.

Millett, M. 1990. *The Romanization of Britain. An Essay in Archaeological Interpretation*. Cambridge.

1995. *Book of Roman Britain*. London.

Milne, G. 1995. *Book of Roman London*. London.

Morris, P. 1979. *Agricultural Buildings in Roman Britain*. Oxford.

Needham, S. and Macklin, M. G. (eds.) 1992. *Alluvial Archaeology in Britain*. Oxford.

Pearson, A. 2002. *The Roman Shore Forts. Coastal Defences of Southern Britain*. Stroud.

2006. *The Work of Giants. Stone and Quarrying in Roman Britain*. Stroud.

Penhallurick, R. D. 1986. *Tin in Antiquity. Its Mining and Trade throughout the Ancient World with Particular Reference to Cornwall*. London.

Perring, D. 1991. *Roman London*. London.

Potter, T. W. and Johns, C. 2002. *Roman Britain*, 2nd edn. London.

Salway, P. 1981. *Roman Britain*. Oxford (reprint 1997), esp. 553ff.

1993. *The Oxford Illustrated History of Roman Britain*. Oxford.

Schrüfer-Kolb, I. 2004. *Roman Iron Production in Britain. Technological and Socio-economic Landscape Development along the Jurassic Ridge*. Oxford.

Scullard, H. H. 1979. *Roman Britain. Outpost of the Empire*. London.

Shotter, D. 1996. *The Roman Frontier in Britain. Hadrian's Wall, the Antonine Wall and Roman Policy in the North*. Preston.

Todd, M. (ed.) 2004. *A Companion to Roman Britain*. Oxford.

Tyers, P. A. 1996. *Roman Pottery in Britain*. London.

van der Veen, M., Livarda, A. and Hill, A. 2008. New Plant Foods in Roman Britain. Dispersal and Social Access, *Environmental Archaeology* 13, 11–36.

Wacher, J. 1995. *The Towns of Roman Britain*, 2nd edn. London.

1998. *Roman Britain*, 2nd edn. Stroud.

Webster, G. (ed.) 1988. *Fortress into City. The Consolidation of Roman Britain, First Century* AD. London.

Index